THE RELIGION OF THE HEBREWS

(To A.D. 70)

GREAT RELIGIONS OF THE EAST

EDITED BY
ERIC S. WATERHOUSE, M.A., D.D.
Professor of the Philosophy of Religion in the University of London.

OUTLINE OF HINDUISM.
F. HAROLD SMITH, D.D.

CONFUCIANISM AND TAOISM.
B. S. BONSALL, M.A., D.LIT., B.D.

SHINTOISM.
A. C. UNDERWOOD, M.A., D.D.

ZOROASTRIANISM.
J. W. WATERHOUSE, B.A., B.D.

OUTLINE OF BUDDHISM.
C. H. S. WARD.

AN OUTLINE OF ISLÂM.
C. R. NORTH, M.A.

THE RELIGION OF THE HEBREWS
C. RYDER SMITH, B.A., D.D.

IN PREPARATION.

THE DAWN OF RELIGION.
ERIC S. WATERHOUSE, M.A., D.D.

JUDAISM.
I. EPSTEIN, PH.D., D.LIT.

THE RELIGION OF THE HEBREWS

(To A.D. 70)

BY

C. RYDER SMITH, B.A., D.D.

Principal of Richmond College, Professor of Theology in the University of London

LONDON
THE EPWORTH PRESS
(EDGAR C. BARTON)
25-35 CITY ROAD, E.C.1

First Edition, 1935

Made and Printed in Great Britain by
A. BROWN & SONS, LIMITED, HULL.

TO

MY COLLEAGUES AT RICHMOND

CONTENTS

EDITOR'S FOREWORD

THE quest for God is one in which all nations have shared. Call Him what they may, all peoples seek God, though they seek not as do we. Yet to understand both their unity with and differences from us must help to closer sympathy and respect. The purpose of this series is not critical nor apologetic but rather is it descriptive. It is that of giving some account, by reference to the scriptures and great teachers of other religions, of the way in which the faiths of the world have faced the same spiritual issues that are ours. In this respect the volumes in this series are intended as a simply written contribution to the work of the Comparative Study of Religions.

E.S.W.

PREFACE

In some ways it is difficult to write a *short* account of the religion of Israel in Biblical times. For one thing the amount of detail accumulated by the prolonged researches of scholars is very great and one has to select. For another there is still difference about the dates of the Old Testament documents and it is impossible to include a discussion of these differences. Yet if one follows the dates of the 'traditionalist' or 'fundamentalist' school, the story of Hebraism is not the same as if one adopts the methods and conclusions of the so-called 'critical' school. Again, the history of religion can only be understood in relation to general history, yet to sketch the story of the twelve or fifteen centuries covered by this book in a few pages is not easy. There are also other smaller but obstinate difficulties. For instance, within both traditionalist and critical schools there are differences of emphasis or of opinion where one must take one side or another.

Under the circumstances a writer can only choose his own way, saying little of other ways. This book follows the findings of the constructive school that is commonly called 'critical.' In other words, I assume that the agreed conclusions of the great mass of scholars to-day about the dates of the documents are correct. For the grounds of their conclusions and for the detailed conclusions themselves I must refer the reader to books on 'Introduction.' Where the exponents of critical or historical conclusions differ among themselves on a subject of any importance I have usually referred to the point of difference, but confined myself to stating my own view. There is a partial exception in the First Chapter.[1] Again, in that chapter I have not thought it necessary to say much about the general history of Israel as told in the Old Testament itself, for this is perhaps its most familiar part.

A few minor points need mention. The study begins with Moses, and not with Adam, since the stories of the Book of Genesis are best treated as giving evidence of the ideas of Israel in post-Mosaic days. Objection could be taken to the name of the book, for many would say that after the fall of Jerusalem in 586 B.C. the term 'Hebrew' should give way to the term 'Jew.' Yet it is not easy to find a name for the religion of Israel in the period covered, and some, at least, would claim that the Judaism of to-day was born in A.D. 70,[2] rather than in 586 B.C. Again, I ought perhaps to state that I have used a capital letter for the word 'God'[3] when using it in a monotheistic way, and for the word 'Prophet' on reaching the time when the Hebrew Prophet rose unmistakably above the prophets of other races. There is no bibliography at the end of the book. Books on the Old Testament are legion and bibliographies can be found in the dictionaries and commentaries or in Messrs. Nisbet's sixpenny *Scripture Bibliography*. There is a bibliography for beginners at the end of *What is the Old Testament?*—another small volume that I have written on a similiar subject, though under a different method. I have ventured to refer to this book here and there as well

[1] pp. 37ff.
[2] Or even in A.D. 135.
[3] And for the words 'He' and 'Him' when they refer to God.

as to others of my books that deal with the Old Testament.[1] Finally, I have tried to treat the subject historically, in harmony with the method of the series. This means that the subjects of revelation or inspiration, and of the authority of the Old Testament for Christians, are omitted. On the other hand, at one or two points in the last chapter, which deals with the period when Christianity arose, I have made no attempt to hide the fact that I am myself a Christian.

It is a pleasure as well as a duty to thank the Rev. Norman H. Snaith, M.A., for reading the proofs and making a number of valuable suggestions, and the Rev. G. A. E. Cornforth, M.A., for drawing up the Indexes.

C.R.S.

[1] *The Bible Doctrine of Society*, *The Bible Doctrine of Wealth and Work*, and *The Bible Doctrine of Womanhood*.

SOME PRINCIPAL DATES

For Chapter I (to *ca.* 800 B.C.):

ca. 1440 or *ca.* 1240		The Exodus.
ca.	1000	The Reign of David.
ca.	930	The Division of the Hebrew Kingdoms.
ca.	850	Ahab and Elijah.

For Chapter II (from *ca.* 800 to 538 B.C.):

ca.	760	The Prophecies of Amos.
ca.	740-695	The Prophecies of Isaiah.
	722	The Fall of the Northern Kingdom.
ca.	626-580	The Prophecies of Jeremiah.
	586	The Fall of the Kingdom of Judah.
ca.	545	The Prophecies of Deutero-Isaiah.

For Chapter III (536 B.C. to A.D. 70):

	536	The Return of Jews under Zerubbabel.
	444	Nehemiah appointed Governor.
	331	Alexander in Palestine.
	165	Judas Maccabæus rededicates the Temple.
	63	The Romans take Jerusalem.
A.D.	70	The Fall of the Temple.

THE RELIGION OF THE HEBREWS

CHAPTER I

PREPARATION—FROM MOSES TO ELIJAH

Civilization was old before Israel was born. Not only so, but when the Hebrews burst into Canaan, that particular land had known civilization for many centuries. While the period when Joshua crossed the Jordan and attacked Jericho is still doubtful, no one puts this before 1600 B.C. and most place it either *ca.* 1400 B.C. or *ca.* 1200 B.C. But Palestine is on the highway from Egypt to the Mesopotamian plain, and in both these great river areas there were civilizations from 5000 B.C. onwards. And between them there was continual coming and going. Again, in the many centuries before 1200 B.C., at one time a Babylonian Empire, and at another an Egyptian, ruled Palestine for generations. It is necessary to rid the imagination of the idea that there is anything in the Old Testament beyond a few vestiges that goes back to 'primitive man' or to 'primeval times.' Some authorities say that there have been creatures that may be called 'men' upon the earth for a million years! In such a perspective the year 1400 B.C. is only of yesterday, and it is not remarkable that competent scholars should say that 'modern history properly begins with the year 1479 B.C.'[1] when an Egyptian king of the *Eighteenth* Dynasty swept over the Plain of the Kishon. Civilization was old when Israel was born.

In the period before Joshua the land of Canaan lay in the midst of four great civilizations. These were the Egyptian civilization to the south-west, the Mesopotamian to the east and north-east, the Hittite to the north, and the Aegean to the west. Writers used to speak only of the first two, but recent archæology has unearthed the others.[2] Geographically Canaan was the focus of the four. It is difficult to say how far each of them influenced the people of Palestine either before or after the coming of the Hebrews, but it is impossible to doubt that the atmosphere of the land, when Joshua broke into it, was the atmosphere of an old, confused and perhaps decaying civilization. It is true that, so far as our records go, the Egyptians and Babylonians did not settle permanently in large numbers. Their occupation was rather like the British occupation of India than of South Africa. Yet their rule must have left deep marks, again like British rule in India. The Bible tells that Hittites settled in the land.[3] The Philistines sprang from the Aegean civilization. There is no need to say that commerce was already very old or that its influence was vast. Palestine, where no great civilization was native, borrowed much from alien culture. If we may judge by parallel instances, it probably borrowed badly. We don't know whether

[1] Oesterly and Robinson, *A History of Israel*, Vol. I, p. 4.

[2] It is possible that it may add a fifth under the term 'Horite.'

[3] Some scholars think that they settled in large numbers; they were neither nomads nor Semites.

to compare it to a reliquary or a sink; no one would compare it to a casket.

Yet the people who dwelt in Canaan did not come, in the main, from any of the four great civilized areas. They came from an area nearer than any of these, the desert. Their forefathers, therefore, had been nomads. For centuries or even millenniums before Joshua, wave after wave of nomads had swept into Palestine out of the desert to the north-east, east and south. In part they may have come because the desert was slowly growing drier and drier, and it was harder and harder to live there. In part, too, they may have come because, compared with the desert at its best, Palestine seemed a land 'flowing with milk and honey.' In any case, they came. The Phœnicians, the Amorites, and finally the Hebrews were successive waves of this immigration. It is doubtful what 'Canaanite' means, but in its narrower sense the name may represent another of the series of irruptions.[1]

The transition from a nomadic to a settled life meant a social revolution. It has been called the greatest social revolution that can befall man. The nomadic life is so distant from ours that we have no one word for its opposite—a settled life. We take it for granted that all men are used to living at a fixed spot. Our distinctions are between the size and culture of the various spots. So our terms are hamlet, village, town, city, metropolis. Hebrew has one term for them all (עִיר)! For through all Hebrew history the nomad roamed the desert at the door, and settled man could not forget the great gulf that lay between

[1] It is used in this book in its wider sense, for all the inhabitants before Israel came.

him and them. And, while we can say little of the religion of the nomad, there are traces that the early Hebrew, even though he was himself settled, thought the nomad life the better way. For instance, the story of Cain and Abel tells how the God of the Hebrews preferred the nomad's offering to the agriculturalist's, and of course agriculture was the habit of settled men. Nomads do not plant vines or olives, and rarely grow corn. It is no accident that Cain 'goes out of the presence of Jehovah' to 'build a *city*,' or again, the story of the Tower of Babel betrays a nomad's horror at the strange ways of a polyglot metropolis. A huge *building* is the epitome of the horror. Nomads do not build. Similarly, Lot falls into a haunt of sin when he betakes himself to the *city* of Sodom. It may be said that it was inconsistent for the Hebrew, when he had himself settled, to pillory 'cities.' It is as inconsistent—and as natural—as it is for the modern Englishman to live in a town and praise the country. Neither the thought nor the practice of a people is ever logically consistent. We shall find other illustrations of this frequently forgotten fact.

When the Hebrews broke into Canaan, it was to practise a Jihad or holy war. This meant that they set themselves to exterminate the more or less mingled earlier races. For instance, they 'death-devoted' every inhabitant of Jericho except the family of Rahab. But, as the Old Testament itself abundantly witnesses, they failed to complete this terrific purpose. There are a few signs that for a while they and the remaining Canaanites lived uneasily side by side in different towns and villages.[1] But by degrees this stage passed into another. Gradually the two races coalesced.

[1] e.g. Jud. xix, 10-14.

This process was the easier as the two peoples talked almost the same language. The need to make a common front against the Philistines perhaps hastened the process, and no doubt intermarriage[1] hastened it still more. Probably in the time of David (*ca.* 1000 B.C.) the process was practically complete.

In this mixed race the Hebrew stock seems to have been dominant, for the god of the one people was the Hebrew god Jahveh.[2] It is impossible to call David a Canaanite. Yet the word 'dominant' needs much modification. The Angles and Saxons were dominant in the areas where they mingled with the Welsh, yet the influence of the latter in the composite race was great. Are the peoples of Spanish America Spaniards or Indians? Probably the Hebrews, dominant though they were, were less numerous than the Canaanites. At any rate the latter contributed largely to the customs and ideas of the combined race. It is often difficult and sometimes impossible to say which elements in the general culture of this mixed people derived from the Hebrews and which from the Canaanites. Some customs, such as circumcision, they shared with other peoples. Some others, such as the three annual Harvest Festivals (the Feast of Unleavened Bread, the Feast of Weeks and the Feast of Tabernacles) do not suit a nomadic but an agricultural people, and probably therefore derive from the Canaanites. The earlier records tell, on the other hand, that the Israelites practised the Passover before they entered Canaan,[3] and its rite of the Shared Lamb suits a nomadic folk. But the number of customs that can confidently be assigned to Israel is

[1] Exod. xxxiv, 16; Ezek. xvi, 3. [2] See pp. 18f.
[3] Exod. xii, 21ff.

disappointingly small. One reason is that the archæological remains of the Canaanites are so far much more numerous than those of the Hebrews. The suggestion has even been hazarded that the narratives of the three Patriarchs, Abraham, Isaac and Jacob, originated with the Canaanites, since many of their stories centre in spots that were sacred to the Canaanites before Israel arrived. This raises, of course, the question of the historicity of the great Three. Their stories are mentioned here to show how difficult it is confidently to ascribe anything to the Hebrews and to the Hebrews alone. If the epic of Jacob, for instance, the Ulysses of Israel, is mainly Hebrew, is there nothing in it of Canaanite origin ?

Yet there are a few things that were undoubtedly Hebrew, or almost certainly so, and these are very important. Moses is one of the few men in history who have made a nation. Moreover he made it in a distinctive way. He found forlorn companies of slaves in Egypt, or in Goshen on its border, and he led them into freedom and nationhood. And the nation that he made lives to-day. This is a unique phenomenon. It is true that, according to our records, these slaves harboured some memories of great ancestors, but without Moses these memories would have perished. It was he who made Israel.

Again, Moses made Israel, spite the Pharaoh and the might of Egypt, because he was the devotee of a particular god. The consonants of this god's name are JHVH. What the vowels were no one knows, for in early Hebrew documents no vowels were written, and the time came when the name was counted so holy that no one ever pronounced it. So the vowels were forgotten. The Greek translators of the Old Testament, followed by the English versions, rendered the name by the phrase 'the LORD,' but this is a title while the word itself is a proper name. In current English the form 'Jehovah' prevails, but its vowels only date from the sixteenth Christian century and are certainly wrong. The form 'Jahveh' (pronounced 'Yahweh') is perhaps the most likely scholarly surmise, and it will be used in this book. Moses' message to his servile kinsmen was 'Jahveh hath sent me unto you.' He himself had met this god among the Midianites,[1] and this suggests that his worship was not at first peculiar to Israel. Recent archæology bears this out. Its evidence, however, is only of antiquarian value. Jahveh has lived in history till to-day because he was the god of Israel. In its conviction it was he who rescued its fathers from Egypt and gave them Canaan. This conviction reverberates in their documents from beginning to end.[2] Alike in their songs, their laws, their prophecies and their histories it is Jahveh who 'brought us out of the land of Egypt.' He was their deliverer. Of such a religious idea this is *the* historical instance. It is impossible to exaggerate the permanence and intensity of its sway among the faithful in Israel.

Yet the deliverance does not stand alone. Moses led the people to the flaming mountain where he had himself met Jahveh, or rather where Jahveh had met him, and there Jahveh and Israel made 'covenant.' The records portray this rather as a renewal of an old covenant than as a novelty, but for 'the children of

[1] Exod. iii.

[2] e.g. Exod. xv; xx, 2; Deut. vi, 20ff; Jud. xix, 30; 1 Kings ix, 9; Hos. xi, 1; Ezek. xx; Psalms cv, cxxxvi; Neh. ix, 6ff.

Israel' it now became an effective thing. The birthplace of Israel is Sinai.

It is easy for us to decry the concept of covenant. Some people like to compare it to a commercial bargain, but this is mere anachronism, for Israel was not a commercial people and did not think in commercial terms. Its covenant with Jahveh should rather be compared to the explicit covenant in marriage or to the implicit covenant of family life. In other words, it was a form of fellowship. Only it was not a fellowship of man with man, but of god with man. It is true that the word 'fellowship,' being modern, refers chiefly to a psychological phenomenon, while a covenant in the period under discussion was defined in terms of outward act, but it was not therefore merely conventional or legal. In those days Israel had hardly begun to be introspective and everything was defined in 'external' terms. The psychological or 'inward' counterpart was none the less there. From the day of covenant at Sinai Jahveh and Israel were one. He was not just the ruler of his people but part of it, as the head is part of the body, or the father part of his family. Jahveh and Israel faced the world together. He was *their* god and they were *his* people. He was as much one with them as Alfred was one with his English. It is commonly said that for Israel Jahveh was a 'living' god, but this is inadequate. Originally all gods were 'living.' It would be quite wrong to use at this stage such terms as 'omnipotence' and 'omniscience,' but in all the records the idea never occurs that Jahveh cannot do anything that he wants to do, or cannot be where he wants to be, or does not know everything that he needs to know. And the thing that he wants to do is to care for Israel. It is his business to 'see Israel through,' and he can and does. Alike in the stories of Moses, Joshua and the Judges, he is Israel's invincible saviour; the human leaders are only his instruments. On the other hand, it is Israel's business to do what Jahveh wants it to do. It sometimes fails to do this, but this does not invalidate the idea, any more than a child's undutifulness to-day invalidates the idea that he ought to be obedient, or a Christian's lapse that he ought to serve Christ. The concept of covenant is consistent and clear.

'Thou shalt worship no other god, for Jahveh, whose name is jealous, is a jealous god.'[1] This quotation is from an early collection of laws and gives us another mark of early Hebraism. The Canaanites were polythcists, and this, as will appear below, in more than one way. While it would not occur to any early Hebrew that Jahveh was the only god, he yet thought that he ought to worship only Jahveh. With other gods he ought to have nothing to do, and they had nothing to do with him. A modern Englishman knows that there are many Parliaments in the world, but he thinks that there is only one that he ought to obey. Once more, the possibility or probability that sometimes an early Hebrew did steal away to another god's shrine, does not invalidate the general concept. To-day there is a technical word for it—monolatry. It is doubtful how far it obtained in ancient times, or in what various forms. The best Old Testament parallel is in a chapter of Judges about Chemosh, the god of the Moabites.[2] But, however common or uncommon it was, it was no Canaanite practice but Hebrew. As

[1] Exod. xxxiv, 14. [2] Jud. xi, 24.

we shall see, it was one of the ideas that cannot survive. It was bound either to degenerate into polytheism, or to ennoble into monotheism. Its importance in the history of religion lies in the fact that in Israel it took the second way. If a single word be sought to describe the religion of the first Israelites, it is 'monolatry.'

The meaning of this concept grows clearer if we consider some of the things that Israel inherited or borrowed. The practice of sacrifice was old long before Moses was born. Its origin, its earliest forms and its original meaning are obscure. But from the first, in some form it was for Israel a part of the *cultus* of Jahveh. Circumcision again, was practised by every race in the environment of Israel except the Philistines, yet for Israel it was a mark of a worshipper of Jahveh. The division of the twenty-eight days of the lunar month into four parts, with the consequent institution of the Sabbath, was older than Israel, yet Israel hallowed the Sabbath to Jahveh. It was the same with the Feast of the Passover. Israel gave it a historical origin of its own that linked it with the great deliverance of Jahveh.[1] Other peoples had prophets, but Hebrew prophets were prophets of Jahveh. Israel borrowed both the story of the Garden of Eden and of the Flood from earlier folklore. Probably the *locus* of both was originally Babylonia, for in the first story the Euphrates is named, and there is archæological, as well as geographical, evidence that the lower Mesopotamian plain was subject to great floods. Again, there are parallel Babylonian stories, 'featuring' Babylonian gods. But when Israel took over the stories, it baptized them into the name of

[1] Exod. xii.

Jahveh. Other instances could be given. Israel, was a great borrower, but often it changed what it borrowed. It subdued it to monolatry. There is another striking instance in its treatment of 'evil spirits.' When one of these came upon a man, the early Hebrew did not say, as so many other races would have said, that he 'had a demon,' it said that 'an evil spirit from Jahveh' had come upon him.[1] And it outlawed magic and witchcraft,[2] for the essence of these is the coercion of gods and spirits, and Jahveh could not be coerced. The story of the witch of Endor gives the point of view.[3] Saul consulted her when 'Jahveh had departed from him,' but he knew that he ought not to do so, as the story itself implies. It was the duty of Israel to worship Jahveh and him only. This is not only explicit in the earliest law-codes,[4] but implicit in the whole story.[5]

Was the concept of Jahveh 'personal' and 'anthropomorphic'? These terms are modern and not ancient, but it is easy to show that Jahveh was thought, like men, to think and feel and will. In other words, he was alive. Whether 'anthropomorphism,' in the sense that he was worshipped under the form of an image, and of a human image, obtained at this time will be discussed later. It is certain that

[1] 1 Sam. xvi, 14; cf. 1 Kings xxii, 19-23.

[2] Exod. xxii, 18.

[3] 1 Sam. xxviii, 3ff.

[4] Exod. xxxiv, 11-17; xxiii, 20-33.

[5] It ought, however, to be mentioned that some scholars hold that, while the monolatrous concept is taught in the oldest extant Hebrew documents (dating about the eighth century B.C.), yet there was an earlier stage when the Hebrew saw no harm in worshipping other gods as well as his national god, and habitually did so. This means that the earliest Hebrews did not need the Canaanites to teach them polytheism, and that the idea that they should only worship Jahveh did not emerge till the time of Elijah or even Amos.

in many ways he behaved like living beings in general, and men in particular. In what other ways could he be thought of at all? But to-day the whole trend of the expert study of the oldest concepts of deity emphasizes the opposite idea—that the divine is 'other' or even 'wholly other' than the human. Professor Otto of Marburg has made the term 'numinous' current to describe this concept. Looking for an analogy to-day he compares it to the 'eerie.' It is something that at once attracts and frightens. It is strange, not familiar. The divine—for at the earliest stage 'god' is too definite and personal a word—is far more unlike man than like him. Or rather, in primitive thought any sense of likeness is implicit; the explicit, the significant, the crucial idea is that he is different. This makes him awe-ful, in the strict sense of the term.

This idea of the 'numinous' has never perished among men. It is not indeed ubiquitous in worship, for men have sometimes taken liberties with their gods, but it has been persistent none the less. To-day, after a rather long eclipse, it is returning upon us, for the 'numinous' becomes at length the 'transcendent.' It is certain that the idea persisted through the long millenniums of early civilization. It is also certain that it obtained in early Israel. The story of Sinai has often been used to illustrate it. The people long to have to do with Jahveh, yet they shudder away from the burning mountain.[1] Another illustration may bring the Hebrew notion even more clearly before a modern mind since we cannot so easily accommodate it to our own ideas.[2] In the days of

[1] Exod. xix, 3-25; xx, 18-21.
[2] 1 Sam. iii-vi; 2 Sam. vi.

Eli we find the Ark at Shiloh. It was a 'numinous' object, for it both guaranteed the presence of Jahveh and marked his separateness. When the Israelites were hard bested in the struggle with the Philistines, they sent for the Ark, and all Israel shouted with the anticipation of victory as Jahveh came into the camp. But another defeat ensued, and both parties thought at the moment that Jahveh and Israel had been beaten together. A Hebrew woman spoke for all her people when she cried 'The Glory has departed.'[1] But it soon appeared that Jahveh was by no means beaten. It was this fact that passed the details of a favourite story from lip to lip in Israel for centuries. The Ark of Jahveh (and, of course, where it was, he was) was set before the god who seemed to have worsted him—but it was not Jahveh but Dagon that did obeisance, his image smashing on the floor. And then a strange pestilence began to spread wherever this alien god went.[2] It had seemed that he could not do as he liked, but this was only seeming. Did he want to go back to his own land? A 'new cart' was brought and two cows were taken from their calves and yoked to it. They will return to their young unless some strange compulsion drives them to the Hebrew hills. The god lays his will upon them, driving with unseen hands. The very animals are aware of it, for they bellow under its coercion. At Beth-Shemesh the same pestilence befalls the over-eager welcome of the Hebrews. The Ark is taken to Kiriath Jearim, and no doubt left alone. In due time David wishes to make his new capital of Jerusalem a city of Jahveh.

[1] 1 Sam. iv, 21.
[2] Probably a form of bubonic plague, if the combination mice *plus* 'hæmorrhoids' *plus* pestilence may be equated with the Indian combination rats *plus* bubos *plus* plague.

Both he and his people think that Jahveh will 'dwell there' if his Ark is there. But at first he seems unwilling to come, for he 'breaks out' upon Uzzah. At the second attempt, David, prophet-wise, dances before Jahveh with all his might. The devotee is trying to induce his god to come with him. And he does come. Throughout the story the *mysterium tremendum* and the *mysterium fascinosum*—to use Otto's words—the awe of the Hebrew before Jahveh and his yearning for him are evident. To use the Old Testament word for the 'numinous,' Jahveh is 'holy.' The root meaning of the Hebrew term seems to be 'religiously separate.' Jahveh is holy, and everything that is separate to him—whether it be a man, as a prophet, or a day, like the Sabbath, or a place, like the spot of the terebinths at Hebron, or a movable coffer, like the Ark—is holy too. If now the concepts of the holy and of covenant be put together, we get a logical contradiction, but a significant fact. For early Israel, Jahveh is at once 'terrible' and 'gracious.'

If Israel was bound to do the will of Jahveh, how was his will to be known? Here several ideas can be traced. It was thought that in 'the old days' Jahveh spoke directly to men as men speak to each other. For instance, Jahveh spoke thus to Adam, to Abraham, and to Moses. But these were extraordinary men. The Holy One did not so speak to the common run of Hebrews. *They* could only learn Jahveh's will through some intermediary. It is obvious how readily such a concept falls in with that of the numinous—of the awfully separate god who yet wishes that Israel should know his will. There were several kinds of intermediaries. Sometimes omens were used, as when David and his men heard 'the sound of a going in the tops of the mulberry trees.'[1] Another intermediary was the 'angel' (literally, messenger). We read, for instance, that 'the angel of Jahveh' spoke to Hagar, to Moses, to Gideon, to Manoah and to Elijah. It is not easy to decide how the angel was related to Jahveh himself. In one of the stories of Abraham, for example, 'three men' visit the Patriarch, and one of them turns out to be Jahveh himself, while the other two are called 'angels.'[2] Here the angels are distinct from Jahveh. Gideon's visitant, on the other hand, is at one point called 'the angel of Jahveh' while at another he appears as Jahveh himself.[3] In a number of other passages the intermediary is a sacred flame. This appears in various forms—as a mysterious moving fire in a story of Abraham,[4] in the 'burning bush' of Moses' first vision, in the 'pillar of fire' in the wilderness, in the burning mountain at Sinai, in the holy fire that covered the Ark in the Temple, and in the 'fire of Jahveh' that fell on Carmel in answer to Elijah's prayer. Perhaps in these early centuries this literal fire was the 'glory' of Jahveh of which we read throughout the Bible. Here again, as with the 'angel,' it is not easy to say whether the flame was Jahveh himself, or only his manifestation. Yet even the 'angel' and the 'glory' were not for ordinary men about their ordinary occasions. For these there were human intermediaries. Here there is variety. Both the judge and the king were thought of as instruments

[1] 2 Sam. v, 23f. The concept of omen may lie behind the story of Balaam. The prophet 'had a donkey and he wouldn't go,' and Balaam interpreted his ass's repeated reluctances to mean that Jahveh resented his errand.

[2] Gen. xviii, 1, 2, 22; xix, 1.

[3] Jud. vi, 11, 14.

[4] Gen. xv, 17.

of the god of Israel. For instance, the phrase for the latter, 'the Lord's anointed'—or, to use the Hebrew terms, the Messiah of Jahveh—implies this.[1] But two other human intermediaries are more prominent. These are the priest and the prophet. At this early stage 'Levite' seems to be a synonym for a priest, or at least for a kind of priest.[2] There were priests who were not of the house of Aaron.[3] In some ancient races all kings were priests, but it is not clear whether this was so in Israel.[4] It is likely that in time to offer sacrifice became a prerogative of priests, but that of old time it had not been so.[5] Yet sacrifice was not a means of getting to know Jahveh's will. To do this the priest used the 'ephod.' What this was we do not know,[6] but it seems clear that with the 'ephod' there went the Urim or sacred lots.[7] The other prominent intermediary is the 'prophet'—earlier called the 'seer,' if one passage may be trusted.[8] There is no reason to believe that 'prophecy,' as it appears in this period, was peculiar to Israel. What was peculiar was that among the Hebrews the prophets were devotees of Jahveh, even as among the Phœnicians they were devotees of Baal. The most obvious sign that men were prophets was a certain religious *afflatus* that sometimes fell upon them. The best Biblical instances of this phenomenon are the pictures of 'Saul among the prophets,' of Micaiah

[1] For the judge see Exod. xviii; 1 Sam. vii, 6.
[2] Jud. xvii, 7-13.
[3] e.g. 2 Sam. viii, 18; xx, 26; cf. 1 Sam. ii, 11, 18.
[4] cf. 1 Sam. xiii, 8ff., with 1 Kings viii, 22ff.
[5] e.g. Gen. iv, 3ff.; Jud. vi, 20-24.
[6] See p. 42.
[7] cf. 1 Sam. xiv, 18f. (R.V. marg.); xxviii, 6; xxx, 7f., and the commentaries on xiv, 41f.
[8] 1 Sam. ix, 9.

and Zedekiah in a story of Ahab,[1] and of the 'prophets of Baal' on Mount Carmel. Prophets haunted 'high places' or wandered from one sacred place to another. They sometimes wandered in groups and one instrument of their ecstatic excitement was music.[2] But this ecstasy was not their only characteristic. They could and did give messages from Jahveh. A 'seer' might be able to tell a man who had lost his asses where they were, for he was 'a man of god.[3] Or a prophet might come to a king with a message from Jahveh, as Samuel came to Saul or Nathan to David. But at least at particular crises there was more than this. If, for instance, any one will read between the lines of the story of the struggle with the Philistines in the First Book of Samuel he will see that twice at least the mingled Hebrew-Canaanite race all but succumbed.[4] It is here that the greatness of Samuel appears. It was he who first made head against the Philistines, and it was he who selected the first two kings, Saul and David, who maintained the struggle and at last brought the desperate issue triumphantly through. After David the Philistines are never again a menace. But Samuel was a prophet of Jahveh; so was Saul at first,[5] and so probably was David.[6] These kings too are called 'The Anointed (Messiah) of Jahveh.' The triumph over the Philistines was the triumph of Jahveh, the Hebrew god. Here was the climax of Samuel's success. A prophet was a devotee of Jahveh, but this did not always merely mean that he danced before his god. No one can reduce Moses or Samuel or Elijah to a dervish.

[1] I Kings xx.
[2] I Sam. x, 5; 2 Kings iii, 15.
[3] I Sam. ix, 6.
[4] I Sam. v; xiii, 15-23; xxxi.
[5] I Sam. x, 6.
[6] I Sam. xvi, 13; cf. 2 Sam. vi, 14.

How did a man come to be a prophet? Not by birth or office.[1] The prophetic *afflatus* might 'come upon' *any* man. In our phrase, the prophet's was an *individual* call. And another significant word emerges here—the word 'spirit.' The 'spirit of Jahveh' was not the monopoly of prophets, unless, for instance, we call Gideon and Samson prophets.[2] None the less, usually the terms 'prophet' and 'spirit' go together. Jahveh chose out this man or that, as it pleased him, for some purpose of his own; he showed his choice by giving him his 'spirit,' and the usual and immediate token of the gift was ecstasy. Yet he was still a 'man of god,' still a prophet, when he was not under ecstasy.[3] And he might at any time declare to men the will of Jahveh. He was an intermediary between god and man, and he was this because he had 'the spirit of Jahveh.' Was the 'spirit' the same as Jahveh himself? One may as well ask whether the sunshine is the same as the sun. The angel, the lot, the fire, the spirit—through these Jahveh reached men. Among them the lot went usually with the priest, and the fire in its regular instance with the Temple; the spirit was the mark of the prophet.

What did Jahveh tell his people to do? Here we have two sources of information. In certain great instances we find Jahveh telling someone to do a *particular* thing, and he does it. For instance, Jahveh tells Abraham to trek to Canaan, and he does so; Jahveh tells Moses to rescue Israel from Egypt, and he does so; Jahveh tells Gideon to attack the Midianites, and he does attack them. But had Jahveh

[1] This is what is implied in 1 Sam. x, 12, by the question 'And who is their father?'

[2] Jud. vi, 34; xiv, 25.

[3] 1 Sam. x, 1ff.; 2 Sam. xii.

any *rules* to give his people to govern the customary conduct of every-day life? Here our chief source of information is three early collections of law.[1] One of these[2] is wholly ritual in content. Various reasons may be suggested, but the fact is clear. Does it follow, however, that early Israel thought that, while Jahveh required a given *cultus*, he took no thought for men's behaviour to each other in daily life? In other words, was his law wholly ritual and not at all ethical? In another of the codes, usually called the 'Book of the Covenant,'[3] we find rules that *we* should call ethical alongside rules that *we* should call ritual, without any hint that the former form one class of laws and the latter another. For instance, in successive paragraphs there are laws about the kindly treatment of the poor and the ritual treatment of God.[4] In other words, Israel did not yet differentiate ethics and ritual. It had so far no idea that there was any distinction between the two. All laws alike were laws of Jahveh—whether they said 'Thou shalt not seethe a kid in its mother's milk' or 'Thou shalt not afflict any widow or fatherless child,' and there was nothing more to say. Yet it is not true that early Hebrew law is wholly ritual. To use a chemical metaphor, so far people saw only water; no one had yet imagined that there were two elements in it, hydrogen and oxygen; yet all the while both were

[1] Exod. xxxiv, 10-26; xx, 22-23, 33; xx, 1-17 (cf. Deut. v, 6-21). The suggestion has been made that the Book of the Covenant (Exod. xxi-xxiii) was originally a code of secular law. I cannot accept this account, not least because Israel seems to me to be a very unlikely exception to the general rule that the law of early peoples is counted of divine origin. The question cannot, however, be discussed here; at any rate the code, as presented in the documents, was for Israel a divine code, whatever its origin.

[2] Exod. xxxiv, 10-26.

[3] Exod. xxi-xxiii.

[4] Exod. xxii, 25-31.

there, awaiting differentiation. There are two signal proofs outside the codes that there was an ethical element in early Hebraism—Nathan's rebuke of David for adultery and Elijah's of Ahab for theft and murder.[1]

There is another ancient code that challenges comparison with the Book of the Covenant, the Code of Hammurabi. It belongs to Babylonia, and is much older than the Book of the Covenant.[2] Many of its laws—like the laws found in the surviving fragments of other ancient races of the Near East—are like those of the Hebrew code. Probably all these codes were based upon customs older than themselves which were common throughout the Old Testament lands. It is often said that if the Book of the Covenant is compared with the Code of Hammurabi, the former has no distinctive character. I cannot agree with this judgement, for it seems to me that the Hebrew code much more markedly takes the side of the poor as over against the powerful. I have shown the grounds of this opinion in detail elsewhere.[3] It is not possible to do so here.

The third code is the Decalogue. Opinion is still very much divided about its date, but there are scholars who think that it *may* be as old as Moses himself.[4] It has often been carelessly spoken of as if its commands were all ethical. On the contrary,

[1] 2 Sam. xii ; I Kings xxi.

[2] Hammurabi's date is *ca.* 1950 B.C. He may be the same as Amraphel (Gen. xiv, 1).

[3] In *The Bible Doctrine of Society*, pp. 56ff. An English translation of the Code of Hammurabi may be found in Hastings' *Bible Dictionary*, Additional Vol.

[4] Apart, however, from enlargements of the Second, Fourth and Tenth Commands. The addition to the Fourth in Exod. xx differs widely from that in Deut. v.

the first four are ritual. The distinction of the code again, is not the originality of the several commands. The Old Testament itself, for instance, assumes that a 'heathen' like the Pharaoh would know that he ought not to commit adultery.[1] The ideas of the code are much older than Moses, or at least almost all of them are. Perhaps the most nearly singular of the Ten is the last, for it passes beyond outward behaviour to motive. But the greatness of the Decalogue is in its selectiveness and its simplicity. It selects the rudiments of all true religion aright. This is why it is on the way to become the universal alphabet of religion for all mankind. It is possible to cavil at its ritual ban on images, for instance, or the literal interpretation of its Sabbath law, but even here the principles that it anticipated—that 'God is spirit' and that man ought to worship Him—are universal. The Decalogue is the Alpha of religion, not its Omega, but it is the right Alpha.

It must not be supposed, of course, that Israel, any more than other peoples, always kept its own laws, but it is clear that in two of these three codes ethical elements lie alongside ritual ones. Hebraism already taught duty to neighbour as well as duty to Jahveh. But who was 'neighbour'? The answer is that he who worshipped Jahveh was neighbour and none else. The outsider—the man who was outside the Covenant—had at least originally, no rights.[2] It is probable that though the last six Commandments in the Decalogue itself are absolute in form, they only applied at first to fellow-countrymen.

[1] Gen. xii, 10ff.

[2] Here again I must refer the reader elsewhere for the grounds of this assertion—*The Bible Doctrine of Society*, pp. 82ff.

To 'spoil the Egyptians,' for instance, was not to steal. The first four Commandments doubtless embody principles that might be applied to the worship of any god, but for Israel, they were laws for the worship of Jahveh. The devout Hebrew cared nothing how other gods were worshipped.

It is now necessary to turn in rather greater detail to the *way of worship* in early Israel—that is, to the ritual or *cultus*—for as usual, *cultus* involved much beside itself. It will be best to begin by asking what the *cultus* of the Canaanites was. We haven't very complete information, but probably we have enough, if the evidence of the Old Testament and of archæology are taken together. These two kinds of evidence do not contradict but confirm each other. As we saw, Israel began with a Jihad against the Canaanites. A passage from one of the early codes will show how this involved a Jihad against their gods—'Take heed to thyself lest thou make a covenant with the inhabitants of the land whither thou goest, lest it be for a snare in the midst of thee: but ye shall break down their altars, and dash in pieces their pillars, and ye shall cut down their Asherim: for thou shalt worship no other god; for Jahveh, whose name is Jealous, is a jealous god.'[1] Archæology bears out the implication that the three commonest *sebasmala*, or objects for use in *cultus*, in Canaanite shrines were the altar, the pillar, and the Ashĕrah.[2] The pillar or obelisk, and not an image, seems to have been the regular emblem

[1] Exod. xxxiv, 12ff.; cf. xxiii, 20ff. 'Asherim,' here and elsewhere, is unfortunately translated 'groves' in the Authorised Version. It is the plural of 'Asherah.'

[2] There were very many others, especially at the shrines of the large cities; see art. 'Canaanites,' in Hastings' *Encyclopædia of Religion and Ethics*. (L. B. Paton.)

of the local 'Baal' or 'Lord,'[1] for this word was, at least for long, a title and not a proper name. The Asherah was a wooden pole, the emblem of a goddess, the wife of the Baal. The words 'Asherah' and 'Ashtart' (or Ashtoreth) are not connected in Hebrew, but the Asherah (probably, at first, a descriptive term, not a proper name) sooner or later became an emblem of Ashtart.[2] It will be noticed that here we have polytheism, in one of its forms—there is a goddess as well as a god. Further, wherever a god and a goddess are found together, the sexual idea takes a prominent place in the concept of the gods, and the *cultus* has a *sexual* element. In other words, we have passed from what we call 'ritual' to what we call 'ethics.' The Canaanite worship, like so many other types of ancient worship, sanctified lust. This fell in readily with the idea that the two gods were gods of fertility, for the action of rain upon the soil was widely taken as parallel to the sexual act. Further, there was a Baal (and an Asherah) for every town and perhaps even for every village. Their power was strictly localized. Here, therefore, there is a second type of polytheism. There was a multitude of 'high places' in the land, and there were as many gods and goddesses as there were 'high places.'[3] To judge by the references in the Old Testament, there were also examples of 'molten gods'—that is, of carved or

[1] 2 Kings iii, 2f.; x, 26f.

[2] It was not the only emblem, for many small images of the latter have been found.

[3] This is, of course, logically inconsistent with the idea that all the Asherim were emblems of one goddess Ashtart, but here is a place where logic did not rule thought. In India there are multitudes of images and multitudes of different gods, yet, if an ordinary Hindu is asked how many gods there are, he will reply 'One.'

'graven' images of wood, overlaid with metal.[1] Much more might be said of Canaanite religion from archæological evidence, but these few facts are the prominent ones in the Old Testament, and they are enough for our immediate purpose.

It has been seen that the Hebrew Jihad was very incomplete and that gradually the Hebrews coalesced with the Canaanites. Did their religions coalesce too? Here we reach one of the chief problems of Old Testament study. The technical term for the amalgamation of cults and religions is 'syncretism,' i.e. 'mixture.' How far did it obtain in Israel? For instance, did it so far obtain that Hebrew monolatry passed into Canaanite polytheism? Were Jahveh and the local Baal so fully identified, village by village, that there were as many gods as there were 'high places'? Again, had Jahveh a goddess as his counterpart, and was his *cultus* sexual? And so on. Was there anything left that was distinctively Hebrew in current religion?

A second set of questions needs also to be asked. Israel dwelt amid other nations, and, as time went on, her life and theirs touched and mingled more and more. From about 1200 B.C. to about 850 B.C., indeed, contact with the two great river areas, Egypt and Mesopotamia, was probably at its minimum, for in these centuries there was no conquering empire in either of these lands, but there were still the nearer and smaller peoples—the Aramæan,[2] the Phœnician, the Philistine, the Edomite, and so on. Did they influence Hebrew religion? In particular, did Israel

[1] cf. Jud. xvii, 4.

[2] That is, the people whose capital was Damascus. 'Aramæan' is a better name for them than 'Syrian,' though the latter term is used in the English Versions.

borrow any of their gods? It will be seen that here was a third way to polytheism. Gods might creep into Israel from outside, and Chemosh of Moab, for instance, might be worshipped by the Hebrews in one shrine as Jahveh was in another. It will be seen that here too syncretism and polytheism, while they are logically distinct ideas, might work together. This was the more likely as the gods of some at least of the other nations—the Phœnicians, for instance—were much like the gods of the Canaanites. How far did the dual process go in the centuries before 800 B.C.?

This brings us to one of the battle-grounds of modern Old Testament scholarship, and it will perhaps be well to state first the chief points of agreement and then those of disagreement.

It is agreed, then, that the ruling phenomenon is the mixture of races, one nomadic and one agricultural, the Hebrew and the Canaanite. It is agreed too that the nomadic race brought into Palestine a religion that was simpler and, to use our word, purer than the Canaanite. It is fairly well agreed, again, that the Hebrew religion was monolatrous and the Canaanite polytheistic.[1] It is agreed that in the latter the two chief objects of the *cultus* were a fertility god and a fertility goddess, and that this meant that the worship was impure.[2] It is agreed, again, that the incoming Hebrews, at least sometimes, took over the 'high places' of Canaanite worship, and that gradually a very large degree of syncretism ensued—that is, that Jahveh and the local Baal were identified and that many of the customs of the Canaanite worship passed to

[1] Yet see footnote on p. 23.
[2] And that it included sodomy, e.g. 1 Kings xv, 12.

the unified race. It is agreed, again, that the influence of neighbour states often led to polytheism.[1] All are agreed, finally, that but for the leadership of the prophets, from Elijah to Ezekiel, the religion of the Hebrews would have gone the same way as the religions of other peoples, and would not have given ethical monotheism to the world.[2]

The subjects on which there is disagreement are more numerous but less important. As usual, to discuss them would take much more space than to state agreed conclusions. The chief question at issue is—*How far* did syncretism and polytheism prevail over the old monolatry ?

The answer partly depends on the findings of archæology and partly on the answer given to another question—How far may we trust the Hebrew documents ? So far as archæology is concerned, at present the results of excavation in Palestine are still small compared with those, say, in Egypt or Babylonia, and what there are, are rather Canaanite than Hebrew. The archæologists, however, are very busy just now, and at any time they may give us discoveries that may settle some of the questions in dispute. As to the reliability of the Hebrew documents, there is fair agreement that somewhere about the time of the Exile[3] a school of editors or redactors took in hand a large number of earlier records—including the documents usually called J and E in the Hexateuch and the earlier stories in the Books of Judges, Samuel and Kings—selected from them such as suited their purpose, edited these with a religiously didactic motive,

[1] Jud. x, 6.

[2] There is a good account of the position in 2 Kings xvii, 8-17.

[3] That is, generations after the period now under discussion, which ends about 800 B.C.

and brought the story down practically to their own time.

Broadly speaking, three several accounts are given of this process of redaction. Under the first the records are taken exactly as they stand, no distinction being made, for instance, between the ancient stories incorporated in the Book of Judges and the editorial 'frame-work' in which they are arranged. Under this account it is taken for granted that all Israel knew from first to last that it was wrong to practise syncretism and polytheism at all. The redactors say that a Canaanitish population remained,[1] and that Israel learnt its evil ways—but they assume that every Hebrew always knew that they were evil, and that Israel as a whole *deliberately* 'sinned' century after century against Jahveh. It is now generally agreed that this account cannot be altogether historical.

Under the second account of the redaction it tends to be assumed that syncretism was universal and complete, and that no one saw anything wrong in it, or made any protest against it. Under this opinion every reference in the documents to any sense of 'sin' in Canaanitish ways is just anachronism. It is claimed, in effect, that Amos (*ca.* 760 B.C.) was the true founder of the distinctive Hebrew faith, and that everything of value in it comes from the Written Prophets. It is not meant that the redactors of the early documents intentionally falsified them, but it is pointed out that, like many other early writers, they lacked the 'historical sense,' that their purpose was not primarily to write history at all, but to teach the truths that *they* saw in history—and that without any due consciousness of what they were doing—they

[1] e.g. Exod. xxiii, 29f.; Jud. ii, 3; ii, 20-iii, 6.

took it for granted that what was obvious to them had all along been obvious to their fathers. Sometimes, indeed, the early documents proved intractable, and, while they altered them on occasion to bring them into agreement with their own convictions, they did not always do so. In consequence many vestiges of earlier ideas survive, and it is suggested that any historical account of early Hebrew religion must be reconstructed from these vestiges, with such outside help as archæology and the study of contemporary cults can offer.

The third account stands midway between the other two. It makes a distinction between editorial comment and historical statement, and claims that these can usually be separated. It claims further that, generally speaking, the historical statements are reliable, and that the evidence of archæology, so far, supports this opinion. It goes on to suggest that, while syncretism went very far, there was always, or nearly always, some protest. In other words, there was a kind of 'godly remnant' from the first, the prophets, devotees of Jahveh and only Jahveh, appearing once and again as its leaders. Yet the battle was all but lost. Without Elijah and Amos and the succeeding prophets it would have been altogether lost. Yet, when these men at last 'turned back the battle at the gate,' they could appeal to an old tradition of protest—they could claim that the popular cult of their day was not the old religion of Jahveh, and that their hearers knew that this was so.

It will perhaps best illuminate the situation if some specimens of the chief difficulties are given. The best focus of the discussion is the question—How far did Israel worship by means of idols? This narrows the issue overmuch if taken alone, for a complex of questions is involved, but it may serve as a kind of key-question. Before it can be discussed a glance must be taken at the findings of to-day about the place of image-worship in ancient religion in general.

As already seen, men do not seem to have begun by thinking that a god is just like a man or an animal. In other terms, the sense of the numinous does not naturally show itself immediately in idolatry. On the contrary, the first solid objects to be used in *cultus* were *natural* objects—the great stone at Bethel, and the great tree or trees at Hebron are Hebrew examples.[1] Similarly early altars were of 'unhewn' or natural stones.[2] These *sebasmata* were not the holy and awe-ful god, nor did they represent him; they were the tokens of the places that were his favourite haunts —of places, therefore, where men were likely to find him.[3] The time came, however, when men thought that some *movable* solid object might guarantee the presence of the god. In Israel the ephod and the Ark were such objects.

Again, the time came when men began to *make* *sebasmata*—that is, to take some natural object and fashion it with tools. These were sometimes idols—that is, representations of animals or men—but not always. The *linga* of Saivism for instance, and the *tope* of Buddhism are not images. Sometimes the two kinds of *sebasmata*, idols and non-idols, occur together—for instance a statue of Shiva is often found in the same shrine as a *linga*, or a statue of the Buddha in the same shrine as a *tope*. Sometimes, again, it seems that

1 e.g. Gen. xxviii, 16ff.; xviii, 1.
2 Exod. xx, 24f.
3 Though he might be met with elsewhere, e.g. Jud. xiii, 3-25.

images were first used to portray the attendants of the god—as the bull and cobra in Saivism—and not the god himself. These attendants might then grow into subsidiary gods—beings with whom it is well to be on good terms, for they may influence the great god. So polytheism might develop in yet another way. Even when the god himself was portrayed as an idol, the worshipper would not think that the image *was* the god. Probably no worshipper has ever thought this. Yet the connexion of the image and the god could be so close that the term 'gods' could be used for the images. Here too, therefore, custom neglects logic. On this showing idols are not original in *cultus*, but creep in as art develops. It is likely, therefore, that their story in Israel will not be simple.

To turn from this focal point to our specimen questions—what was the *ephod*? Sometimes, at any rate, it was a solid object[1]; was it an image? Does the story of Gideon's ephod[2] prove that it was, or is there here, as in the early Laws,[3] just a protest against a 'molten' *sebasma* of any kind? Another *sebasma*, the *teraphim*, was used in household *cultus*—was it an image? If it was, it would follow that even so devoted a worshipper of Jahveh as David was an idolater[4]—yet the story does not quite require this.[5] If it were an image, it might, of course, be an image of Jahveh.

To pass to the Temple, it is clear that in building it Solomon borrowed alien ways. For instance, the

[1] e.g. Jud. viii, 16f. Its relation to the 'linen ephod' is obscure.

[2] Jud. viii, 27.

[3] Exod. xxxiv, 17.

[4] 1 Sam. xix, 13.

[5] I have given reason for this in the *Holborn Review* for July and October, 1930.

style of architecture was Egyptian,[1] and there were undoubtedly 'molten' *sebasmata* within it—the *cherubim*, for instance—but was there an image of Jahveh himself? And was the 'brazen serpent' that Hezekiah destroyed,[2] this image? Or was this at first merely an emblem of an attendant on Jahveh, borrowed from the Canaanites, with an appropriate Hebrew legend attached.[3] What were the original contents of the Ark? An image of Jahveh, or some natural stones from Sinai,[4] or a copy of the Decalogue itself as the records state? Does the protest in 1 Kings viii, 9, *imply* the opposite of what it states? What is the ground of the protest there?

Again, was Solomon a polytheist? There is little doubt that, with the triumph of the Hebrews over the Philistines, there would go a reinforcement or revival of the cult of the Hebrew god, yet we read that Solomon built a number of shrines to alien gods for his alien wives.[5] It is true that he built them well outside Jerusalem, and it may be that they were used chiefly by foreigners frequenting the capital, but they lasted for two hundred years and more.[6]

When we reach the story of the Divided Kingdoms, we find that the redactors seem to rely chiefly on two sources—the 'books of the chronicles' of the kings of both realms and certain 'prophetic narratives.' The former would not be histories of the *people*, in our sense of 'history,' but annals of the kings. The redactors,[7] in selecting from these annals, are chiefly interested in the kings' attitude to the *cultus*. From this point of view they divide them all, from Rehoboam

[1] Perhaps derived indirectly through Tyre.
[2] 2 Kings xviii, 4.
[3] Nums. xxi, 8f.
[4] cf. 2 Kings v, 17.
[5] 1 Kings xi, 5-8.
[6] 2 Kings xxiii, 13.
[7] cf. pp. 86ff.

and Jeroboam to the Fall of Jerusalem[1] into four classes[2]—there are two altogether good kings (Hezekiah and Josiah); there are other good kings, all in Judah, who fall short of the redactors' ideal only in tolerating the local 'high places'; there are two types of evil monarchs—the worst, like Ahab and Athaliah, introduce alien gods, with separate temples,[3] alongside Jahveh; the others, whose examplar is 'Jeroboam, the son of Nebat,' sin, in the main, by syncretism—for Jeroboam's two bulls, at Bethel and Dan, represent a god who could be thought of both as Jahveh[4] and as the Baal of the Canaanites. What are the ideas that lie behind this fourfold classification?

Again, are the redactors altogether wrong in representing the Son of Nebat as introducing something new into Jahvism when he set up his lordly bulls and gave Jahveh an image? Or was he now only officially approving and establishing a form of cult that had long been current among the mingled Hebrew-Canaanite race?[5] We read of two prophetic protests against Jeroboam's act[6]—are they wholly unhistorical? Some claim that the story of Aaron's Calf arose as a protest against Jeroboam's policy—but even on this showing it is a protest. On the other hand—if we may trust the parts of their stories that survive—Elijah and Elisha, while they fling themselves against Ahab's alien cult, make no protest against the Son of Nebat's bulls, and Elijah himself uses a high place on Carmel.

[1] That is, both in this period and in the next.
[2] Hoshea (2 Kings xvii, 2) might be counted a fifth.
[3] 2 Kings x, 21; xi, 18.
[4] 1 Kings xii, 28. 1 Kings xiv, 9, probably represents a later point of view—cf. 2 Kings x, 28f.
[5] The leaven of Canaanites was specially large in the North, e.g. Jud. 1.
[6] 1 Kings xiii, 1-32; xiv, 1-20; cf. xvi, 1-7.

When the redactors name the Asherah they give the impression that while they thought it the uttermost enormity, in Israel it was an *occasional* enormity;[1] is this bad history? In the ordinary worship of the ordinary Hebrew was there a goddess alongside Jahveh? And did the Hebrews regularly follow the custom of religious lust that went with the worship of the Mother-goddess? A story of the days before their fathers broke into Canaan tells that they learnt the habit from the Moabites at Baal-Peor,[2] but this was in the worship of Moabitish gods and Moses punished the sin with death. There is no doubt that the custom did recur, and that under Rehoboam it was followed in its worst form at the 'high places' in the South,[3] but the redactors tell that Asa put an end to this;[4] were they altogether wrong and did the custom run always, even under good kings in the South?

There is also the evidence of two other kinds of documents. At least two short law-codes belong to this period and became more or less authoritative.[5] No doubt their prohibitions of Canaanite *cultus* imply that it sometimes occurred in Israel, but how often? To prohibit murder by law to-day means that it occurs, but not that it is frequent. Finally, to pass beyond our present period, there is the witness of the Written Prophets. To take one instance, Isaiah, who began to prophesy at the end of the long reign of one of the Deuteronomists' good kings,[6] cries 'The whole head is sick and the whole heart faint. From the sole of

[1] e.g. 1 Kings xv, 13; xvi, 33; 2 Kings xiii, 6.
[2] Nums. xxv, 1-5. The story about Phineas (vv. 6-15) belongs to a later document.
[3] 1 Kings xiv, 24.
[4] 1 Kings xv, 12.
[5] See pp. 31ff.
[6] Isa. vi, 1.

the foot even unto the head there is no soundness in it; but wounds and bruises and festering sores.'[1] If this were so, what of the good kings of Judah? The Written Prophets represent the ills of Israel as ancient.[2] Are they wrong?

There is, therefore, a medley of phenomena, but is it not natural that there should be? If any one were to write the history of religion in Britain from Wyclif to the present day, could he reduce it to logic and simplicity? Especially if all the materials he had were annals of the policies of kings, some stories about such men as Wyclif and Knox, and some collections of sermons by such preachers as Latimer and Bunyan and Whitefield? Yet perhaps a provisional conclusion may be suggested. It would be that for the mass of the people the process of the passing of monolatry into syncretism and polytheism went on unresisted and largely unnoticed—that it went further in the north than in the south and east—and that, so far as men took note of it at all, there were several kinds of reaction to it. Among these some may be discerned—there were the Rechabites, the ultra-conservatives, who refused even to pass from the old nomad ways to Canaanitish agricultural life;[3] there were the prophets, who, in varying degrees, resisted the process of change; among the kings there was a variety of policy; at least sometimes and perhaps always the better among them in the south were supported by the priesthood of the Temple[4]; on the whole Israel was going the way of other nations; under Jezebel in the north and Athaliah in the South, the final stage threatened.

[1] Isa. i, 5f.
[2] See further on pp. 61f.
[3] 2 Kings x, 15, 23; Jer. xxxv, 6ff.
[4] 1 Sam. ii, 35; 2 Kings xi.

What was this final stage? Neither queen, at least at first, proposed to abolish the worship of Jahveh, for both called their children by names that included His name.[1] Both rather sought to set shrines of the Syrian Baal[2] alongside those of Jahveh in Israel. In other words, there was here no occasional and illicit practice of polytheism, but a deliberate attempt to make the Hebrews wholesale into polytheists. Many seem to have welcomed the attempt,[3] yet there seems also to have been opposition, headed by the prophets, and in consequence of this the party of the two queens destroyed many of Jahveh's shrines and persecuted his prophets.[4] If the attempt had succeeded, Israel would have been no more than one more little race of antiquity. But the crisis produced the man. Elijah fronted Jezebel. It was not with syncretism that he took issue but with polytheism. On Carmel, in answer to Jezebel's 'Baal *and* Jahveh,' he replied 'No, Baal *or* Jahveh.'[5] In other words, monolatry faced polytheism and prevailed.

Yet it was not on Carmel that the victory was really won but at Horeb, for Jezebel defied Carmel.[6] Even on Horeb only a beginning was made, yet it was the beginning of a decisive movement. It is well, therefore, to study carefully its story.[7] Horeb had been the birthplace of Israel; now a single man fled there to tell Jahveh that he no longer had a people. Elijah thought that his worship was dead. The theophany that followed is one of the most famous

1 The termination -iah and the prefix Jeho- are forms of 'Jahveh.'
2 Now a proper name, as in Phœnicia, Jezebel's home.
3 e.g. 1 Kings xix, 14.
4 1 Kings xviii, 3f., 30; xix, 14.
5 1 Kings xviii, 21.
6 1 Kings xix, 2.
7 1 Kings xix.

examples of the numinous in history. Jahveh is not in the fire, or the whirlwind, or the earthquake, but in a 'sound of gentle stillness.' And there our interest usually ceases. The details that follow, about Elisha and Jehu and Hazael, seem an anti-climax. In reality they mark a decisive point in Hebrew religion. It is not so much that there was anything quite novel in the revelation, but there was a new emphasis. In religion emphasis is sometimes everything. First and chiefly, Jahveh is now thought of primarily as a god of history rather than a god of marvel. He had of course been the god of Hebrew history before, but, from Moses onwards, He had aided and saved Israel chiefly by marvels. It is not that marvel ceases, but it dwindles in importance. There are marvels in the story of Elisha, but they are mainly marvels domestic to the prophets, and it was not by them, but by the rebellion of Jehu at Elisha's instigation, that Jahveh crushed Jezebel. After Elisha, miracle is rare in prophetic story.[1] He and Jehu and Hazael seem to make history, but it is really Jahveh who makes it through them. The concept that Jahveh is the active master of history is dominant with the Written Prophets. It begins to dominate with Elijah on Horeb. And here continuous, normal history is meant, not occasional historic wonder, as in the Exodus.

The second idea readily follows. Jahveh has a tool at hand to scourge Israel for its sins. Hazael, of Aram, is to be the scourge. The Book of Kings shows how effectively he filled the *rôle*. But the significant point is that he is a *foreigner*, and no worshipper of

[1] For its chief apparent instance, the destruction of Sennacherib's army, see p. 67.

Jahveh at all. There is here a cloud like a man's hand. It grew into the great doctrine that Jahveh controls all nations, and not merely Israel, as we shall see in the next chapter.

Thirdly, there is in the story of Horeb a word whose root is the same as the word translated 'remnant.'[1] Hitherto the current concept had been that all Israel was Jahveh's, and Elijah had striven desperately on Carmel to carry all Israel with him. As seen above, probably Israel had long been at variance with itself in religion, but now the Prophets recognize that they can only hope to lead a minority. Once and again a Prophet may seem for a moment to rally the whole people—for instance, Isaiah in the crisis of Sennacherib—but this is rare. More and more it appears that only a 'remnant' will follow. But for Jahveh's purpose a remnant will suffice. Here, again, there is the little seed of a great harvest—'I leave me seven thousand in Israel.'[2] The preparation for the unique achievement of the Prophets is complete.

[1] The word 'leave' in 1 Kings xix, 18.

[2] There is no space here for the story of Athaliah's parallel failure in Judah (2 Kings xi). There the protagonist of Jahveh is not a prophet but a priest, and 'the people of the land' are definitely on his side.

CHAPTER II

CONSUMMATION—THE GREAT PROPHETS

THE two great names in the period just described are Moses and Elijah. The first founded Hebraism; the second saved it from the polytheism that befell all other peoples. The danger, as we shall see, did not end with Elijah, but after him there was always protest against it, and for the 'remnant' of Israel—and it was the 'remnant' that gave monotheism to the world—there was always effective protest. Elijah's work, however, had been conservative rather than progressive. He refused the wrong, popular and easy way of change, but he hardly led at all along the right way. That *rôle* fell to Amos. He lived about a hundred years after Elijah—that is, about 760 B.C.—and he is the first of a series of Prophets who are the chief glory of Hebrew religion. The line lasted for about two centuries. Its chief names are Amos and Hosea, Isaiah and Micah, Jeremiah and the unknown author of Chapters Forty to Fifty-five in our Book of Isaiah, called for convenience Deutero-Isaiah.[1] In part the Book of Ezekiel belongs to this period, in part to the next. There are also the brief oracles of Zephaniah and Nahum,[2] and perhaps of

[1] i.e. Second Isaiah.

[2] There is general agreement that a large part of the books ascribed to these nine Prophets do belong to this period. Some experts are doubtful about Ezekiel. For details readers are referred to books on 'Introduction.'

Habakkuk. In addition there is the work of the Deuteronomic school of writers.

We have no documents that purport to have been written by such earlier Prophets as Elijah and Elisha. We have documents *about* them but none *by* them. From Amos onwards the position is almost exactly reversed. In the Books of Kings—which only give eleven or twelve chapters to the present period—none of the Prophets in our present Old Testament canon is named, except Isaiah. In the much later Books of Chronicles there are passing references to Isaiah and Jeremiah, but that is all. The reasons for this silence may be debated, but in any case it is there. What we have is not the history of these Prophets, but collections of their oracles or sermons.

While our historical books pay so little attention to the Prophets, it is plain that someone valued their oracles, or they would not have been preserved at all. Who took the trouble to write them down and how were they copied and recopied through the centuries that followed? We have little direct evidence. There is a very interesting story of the way in which many of Jeremiah's oracles came to be written down,[1] and Isaiah has a reference to his 'disciples' which may imply that they kept copies of some of his words,[2] but there is little other evidence. We can only suppose that originally either the Prophets themselves wrote down some of their oracles or that there were those among the 'godly remnant' who did so. Of the people who copied and recopied them during the next few centuries we know nothing. Here, of course, these books are only like many other ancient books. In the centuries after the Exile, however, as we shall see,

[1] Jer. xxxvi. [2] Isa. viii, 16.

Israel fell in love with the idea of a 'Canon'—that is, of a collection of authoritative books—and the question inevitably arose, 'Which books is the Canon to include?' By the second century B.C. the answer had come to be 'Not only the Law, but the Prophets.' So far as we can tell, the Scribes, who collected the Canon, had many Prophetic manuscripts before them, for of course it was not possible to gather large numbers of documents into a single volume as a modern printer does, with his thin paper and small type. Indeed, the 'codex,' or book of our kind, was not yet invented. The Scribes had to deal with multitudes of *rolls* of varying size. Some of these seem to have borne names, but some seem to have been anonymous. The Scribes, therefore, arranged them as best they could, assigning the anonymous oracles to such Prophets as seemed to them most likely. They may have had evidence that has now perished, but there is no reason for supposing that they were infallible. Modern scholars have examined the Prophecies so arranged, and in quite a number of instances have come to the conclusion that the Scribes made a mistake. For instance, it is unlikely that oracles that name Cyrus and presuppose the historical situation of his times, were written by Isaiah, who lived about two centuries earlier. Scholars are agreed in the great majority of their findings, though naturally there is still dispute on some points. This is, of course, only the most famous instance of a process that is used with many ancient documents. Happily the results of scholarship leave us with quite enough oracles, period by period and Prophet by Prophet, to give us the main message both of the Prophets in general and each Prophet in particular.

For the Deuteronomic documents we need to turn to the story of Josiah's Reformation.[1] In the middle of the period now in question there fell the reign of Manasseh. This lasted for about half a century and marks the nadir of Hebrew religion in the South.[2] This king, unlike Athaliah,[3] introduced the worship of 'other gods' into the Temple itself.[4] It appears, however, that he did not refuse to worship Jahveh, for his grandson, Josiah, who was six years or so old when he died,[5] bore a name that included Jahveh's. What Manasseh did was to worship other gods alongside Jahveh in the same shrine and to use in it rites that had large and dominant Canaanite and Babylonian elements. In other words, under Manasseh syncretism and polytheism both reached their climax. When, however, Josiah undertook to restore the worship of Jahveh, presumably as it had obtained in the reign of his great-grandfather Hezekiah, there was a priest of Jahveh at hand to help him. His name was Hilkiah, and, *mutatis mutandis*, he played the part that Jehoiada had done under Joash. In the course of the purification of the Temple he came to Shaphan, the civil officer in charge, and said 'I have found the book of the Law in the house of Jahveh'[6] and Josiah at once took this book as the basis of his Reformation. What book was it? While there is dispute on the point, the majority of scholars say that it was a large part of our Book of Deuteronomy.[7] The chief reason is that Josiah's Reformation corresponds with the commands of Deuteronomy. What was the origin of this book of Hilkiah's?

[1] 2 Kings xxiif.
[2] *ca.* 695-641 B.C.
[3] p. 44.
[4] 2 Kings xxi, 4f.
[5] cf. 2 Kings xxii, 1 with xxi, 10.
[6] 2 Kings xxii, 8.
[7] Chaps. xii- xxvi, at least.

There is no doubt that there were earlier books among the Hebrews, for even in the time of Moses, writing was already old. This, of course, does not mean that it was common, but that there was a class, probably quite a small class, of scribes. Among many peoples these were priests, and the collections of books were often kept at shrines. There is some slight direct evidence that this was so in early Israel.[1] But, again, these chapters in Deuteronomy consist almost entirely of laws. There are hints that in early Israel as elsewhere, when legal 'cases' arose that could not be settled by appeal to old custom, they were often taken to Levites or priests for decision.[2] Did this custom altogether cease when the kingship arose? The king was supreme judge in all Eastern states, but usually he delegated large parts of this task, as it was impossible for him personally to cope with its volume.[3] As we have seen, there were at least two earlier collections of laws in Israel.[4] The code of Deuteronomy repeats many of their edicts, enlarges some and adds others. Again, almost all its edicts refer, not to life in such cities as Jerusalem, but in villages. The surmise is not far off that the kings in Jerusalem delegated 'cases' of disputants from the villages to the priests of the Temple, and that in the code of Deuteronomy we have the slowly growing record of their decisions, based on precedents derived from still earlier codes. When, therefore, Hilkiah was called to assist Josiah in his Reformation, he knew that there had been a record of the laws of Jahveh in the Temple, and in due course it was found.

[1] Josh. xxiv, 26.

[2] Exod. xxii, 8; 1 Sam. ii, 25; (cf. vii, 15-17); Deut. xvii, 8ff.

[3] cf. 2 Sam. xv, 2ff. [4] p. 31.

It represents all its laws as going back to Moses. It is very unlikely that this was literally so, but it may well be that Hebrew Law was like an oak that had grown from an acorn that Moses planted. Certainly the code was counted very old in Josiah's day and, to pursue the metaphor just used, the tree was old, though it had not ceased to put forth new leaves.[1]

The work of the Deuteronomists did not cease with Hilkiah's discovery. Probably further laws were added, and older laws developed and sometimes amended. Nor were the Deuteronomists content with laws. They turned also to history. There were two documents, partly law and partly history, which seem to have been already so far authoritative that the Deuteronomists did not much alter them. These are the so-called 'Jahvist' and 'Elohist' documents in the first six books of our Bible.[2] Possibly they wove these into a single whole, but there they stayed. It is from these that quotations have been made in the earlier chapter. For the centuries after Joshua too there seem to have been early documents available. Here the Deuteronomists allowed themselves more license. Our Books of Judges, Samuel and Kings are redactions of earlier documents by Deuteronomic editors. Reference has several times been made in the last chapter to these redactions. *We* call these books, with parts of the Pentateuch, 'historical,' but it was not history proper that the Deuteronomists tried to write. They were fundamentally religious teachers, and they presented history as teaching. Their subject can be readily stated—

[1] There is much debate about details, for which the reader is referred to books on Old Testament Introduction. The above seems to the present writer the most likely account.

[2] Called technically J and E.

they were always preaching on the text that Jahveh has blessed and will bless a loyal Israel, and has punished and will punish a disloyal Israel. The splendid piece of oratory, for instance, in the Twenty-eighth Chapter of Deuteronomy is an eloquent exposition of this one message. It is probable that the Deuteronomists carried on their work into the period of the Exile. Their books are quite unlike the oracles of the Prophets of the time—for one thing, they are the slow product of a school, not the immediate utterance of a single man—but they belong to the same two centuries. For this period, therefore, we have the advantage of contemporary documents.

It is not possible to understand the Prophets except with the background of the history of the time. As we have seen above,[1] Palestine was the focus of a great part of the ancient world, and in particular, to change the figure, it was the bridge between two great river areas, the land of the Nile and the land of the Euphrates and Tigris. Both these were the seats of a very ancient civilization. Both were the natural seats of empire. Frequently there were powerful empires in both areas and there was tension or strife between them. In such strife their frequent meeting ground was Palestine. Usually, therefore, the land that lies between the Desert and the sea—part of which we call Palestine—was ruled either by an Egyptian or a Mesopotamian overlord. The era between Joshua and Elisha is the great exception. During the period covered by the last chapter the piece of the world that was peopled by Hebrews, Arameans, Moabites, Philistines and so on, was more nearly isolated politically than it has ever been before

[1] pp. 13ff.

or since. In the main, its story is the story of the relations between these small peoples, and hardly at all of their relation to the larger world. About the time of Ahab, however, it began to be clear that this period was over. A great empire, the Assyrian, arose in the northern part of the Mesopotamian plain, and began to threaten the 'Westland,' as the Assyrians called the stretch of fertile land between the Desert and the Mediterranean. At the first threat the kings of the small peoples, Ahab among them, made some kind of pact and unitedly opposed the Assyrian. A battle, unnamed in the Bible, was fought at Karkar (854 B.C.). The Assyrian kings' clay records declare it to have been an Assyrian victory—yet the Assyrians withdrew. None the less, Jehu and his immediate successors paid tribute to Assyria, and tribute proved the prelude to annexation. The little kingdoms of the 'Westland' failed to combine a second time, and the Assyrian conquered and annexed their lands one after the other. They began with the peoples nearest their own homeland, and this gave Israel a breathing-space. In this interval the outward prosperity of the Hebrews reached a high level—in the north probably the highest since the division of the kingdoms. But it was a short-lived prosperity. One day Amos saw 'a basket of summer fruit,'[1] and he made it a parable, for the summer fruit of those lands is ripe to-day and rotten to-morrow. 'The times were ripe and rotten ripe for change.' In 732 B.C. Aram fell to rise no more. A similar fate befell Northern Israel ten years later. At this time Judah escaped, in part because she submitted to tribute, in part because Assyria was busy elsewhere.

[1] Amos viii, 1.

The power of Assyria lasted between two and three centuries. Then Babylon, in the south of the Mesopotamian area, always restive, rebelled. An invasion of barbarians—the bane of civilized realms for millenniums, whether in Mesopotamia, Egypt, China, Greece, or Rome—also weakened Assyria. A new power, the Median, arose in the mountains east of Mesopotamia. In 612 B.C., Nineveh fell, and a few years later all was over with Assyria. The 'Westland,' however, did not regain its independence. There was only a change of masters. Babylon and Egypt for a moment disputed the entail of the Assyrian power, and then it fell to Babylon. And with the coming of this Second Babylonian empire the Kingdom of Judah passed away. After a series of small struggles and ineffective intrigues Jerusalem fell in 586 B.C. and the chief men of the south were carried captive. Yet Babylonian power was short-lived. Media, in spite of various vicissitudes, waxed stronger and larger, until it stretched round from the centre of Asia Minor to the eastern shore of the Persian Gulf. Then one of the great men who make history emerged from one of its minor States. This was Cyrus. He may be fairly matched with Cæsar. He made an empire much larger than any we have yet named. It reached from Central Asia to the Aegean. Just after his time it annexed Egypt. Babylon fell into Cyrus' own hands in 538 B.C. This meant that its province of Palestine fell to him too. Our period ends just before this event. It will now be clear that its two centuries were a stirring time. The little peoples of the 'Westland' were no longer isolated; they were caught in a whirlpool of empires. It was at the crisis of this stirring time that the Prophets appeared—Amos and Hosea, Isaiah and Micah, when 'the Assyrian came down like a wolf on the fold'; Zephaniah and Nahum, Jeremiah and Ezekiel, when Nineveh fell and Babylon prevailed; Deutero-Isaiah as Cyrus was steadily rising to wider sway. Again and again in Israel the man matched the moment. In the realm of politics the Hebrew was insignificant; in the nobler realm of religion he won a victory that remains to-day.

What of the internal state of the two little Hebrew kingdoms? As has been seen, in the first decades of our period there was a brief burst of prosperity, under Jeroboam II in the North and Uzziah in the South. After this the political story is of unrelieved gloom. The struggle of empires hardly admits of the prosperity of little peoples. Invading and conquering armies often swept through the 'Westland.' Even when there was local peace, the costs of empire and war had to be paid, and it was paid by the subject peoples. Manasseh, for instance, maintained his throne for half a century by submission to Assyria, and submission meant grinding tribute. As always happens in such stories, ultimately the cost of empire and war fell on the poor. The cry of the oppressed peasantry went up and up into 'the ears of the Lord of Hosts,' and the Prophets gave His answer. In the North, after the Fall of Samaria in 722 B.C., the Assyrian 'carried captive' the 'higher classes' and brought in settlers from other parts of the empire. This is just an instance of the cruel policy of 'deportation' that has so often been pursued in the East. Yet its purpose was not cruelty for its own sake. It was an attempt to eradicate the sense of 'nationality' by the mingling of peoples, and it usually succeeded. No doubt many of the Hebrew peasantry were left in 'Ephraim,' and ultimately amalgamated with the new settlers. This mingled people apparently emerge later as 'the Samaritans,' but for this period they do not count. After 722 B.C. interest centres in Judah. What of the current religion of these two centuries? It has been seen that Elijah and Elisha's polemic was against the polytheism of Ahab and not against the syncretism of Jeroboam I. They have nothing to say, for instance, against the bulls at Bethel and Dan. With the victory of Jehu they won their own battle, and the worship of foreign gods, whether it lurked here and there or not, was never again the practice of a Northern king. According to the Books of Kings all the successors of Jehu sinned not after the manner of Ahab but after that of the son of Nebat.[1] They were syncretists rather than polytheists. The testimony of the two Prophets of the North, Amos and Hosea, does not contradict this, for their chief animus, in the realm of ritual, is against Canaanite syncretism, not outright polytheism. When the Northern Kingdom ended, however, the mingled people of this bit of the Assyrian Empire betook themselves again to polytheism. At least this was so if we may trust the only evidence we have, the account of an enemy.[2] Here another route to polytheism appears—the immigrants worshipped Jahveh, since he was 'the god of the land,' and along with him the gods that they had brought from their old countries. For the century and half during which the Kingdom of Judah survived, this worship was active a few miles north of Jerusalem.[3]

[1] See p. 44, and footnote 2 there.
[2] 2 Kings xvii, 24-41.
[3] In 2 Kings xxiii, 15-20, however, the gods of the immigrants are not named.

It has already been suggested that in the story of the South it is very difficult to harmonize the testimony of the editors of Kings and the Prophets.[1] According to the former, between 778 and 586 B.C. there were four good kings and seven bad ones, the good claiming the greater part of the earlier of these two centuries and the bad of the later. The seven bad kings 'go the whole hog'—with Manasseh as chief villain, they equal the old enormities of Ahab in the North. The only differences are that, as already shown, they make the Temple itself the headquarters of polytheism and they prefer to borrow gods from Assyria and Babylon rather than from Phœnicia. Of the four 'good' kings two tolerate the local 'high places,' like the other 'good' kings of Judah since Rehoboam, while the other two, Hezekiah and Josiah, are the Deuteronomic redactors prime favourites, for they seek to destroy the 'high places' and to concentrate the worship of Jahveh in a purified Temple at Jerusalem.[2] Isaiah, on the other hand, declares that in Judah only a 'very small remnant' is faithful to Jahveh.[3]

It is possible to claim that Isaiah's oracles of this sort belong to the reign of 'bad' Ahaz and not of 'good' Hezekiah, who succeeded him, yet, even so, it seems incredible that this universal disease was altogether the product of Ahaz' sixteen years of rule, especially as it followed a century of 'good' kings. It is perhaps impossible to harmonize the two accounts, but some things may be said in mitigation of the difficulty. It is true of Isaiah, as of Amos and Hosea, that his denunciations of idolatry and current ritual in general may be applied to the syncretism of the 'high places,' where the Hebrew Jahveh was assimilated to the

[1] pp. 43ff. [2] See pp. 86ff. [3] Isa. i, 9.

Canaanite Baal, rather than to the cult of foreign gods. This harmonizes with the Deuteronomists' condemnation of the 'high places,' but at least it seems clear that, when they say that a king did 'that which is right in the eyes of Jahveh,' they mean at least that in the *Temple*, which stood alongside the palace, he withstood syncretism. As for the rest of Judah, 'good' kings may have failed to carry the village priests with them. For, while it is true that in the East the rule *cujus regio, ejus religio* is universal, it is true that even in the East rulers have never been able to enforce it completely. Again, while it is true, as we shall see, that Prophets and Deuteronomists alike were interested both in ethics and ritual, the *chief* pre-occupation of the Prophets was with ethics, and of the Deuteronomists with ritual—so that a Prophet from his point of view might declare that all was wrong, even under a 'good' king like Uzziah, while a Deuteronomist from his point of view might think that on the whole the situation was not unsatisfactory. In how many other instances do the accounts of given periods, even when given by competent judges, vary greatly? To-day there are two very different accounts current of Victorian England. The chief ultimate difference, too, relates to the two reigns of Hezekiah and Josiah, and even on the Deuteronomists' own showing, any good worked by these two devotees of Jahveh vanished like smoke when they died. The conclusion is inevitable that, so far as the great mass of the people were concerned, both in the North and the South, the Hebrew in this time of the clash and mingling of peoples, was going the same way as all the rest. Without the Prophets all Israel would have taken the broad way of nonethical polytheism, which was so easy as to be nearly inevitable at the time, but which ultimately led, as all polytheism leads, to the decay of religion.

The Babylonians captured Jerusalem in 597 B.C., and again in 586 B.C. when they annexed little Judah to their empire. On both occasions they practised the policy of deportation. On the whole, the common people were left in Palestine, while the leading men of all sorts[1] were carried captive. The former seem, at least for a time, to have worshipped on the site of their ruined Temple,[2] but a century and a half later the city still lay in ruins,[3] and the history of these survivors is hardly known at all and of little importance. It was different with the exiles. No doubt many, as always in such deportations, perished on the long march to Babylon and other parts of the East, but the survivors, while they were forlorn and helpless, do not seem to have been persecuted. There is a psalm that bewails their hard lot,[4] but it does not tell of anything worse than scorn.[5] But now a strange thing happened. Usually, as we said, exile slew nationality. Probably it did so with many Jews, and of them we have no history; they just disappeared in the surrounding peoples. But others clung to their nationality—or rather, in the characteristic way of the best of the Hebrew race, they clung to their religion, as being the core of their nationality. For them there was just one choice—keep separate or perish—and they elected to keep separate. To worship

[1] 2 Kings xxv, 18-22.
[2] Jer. xli, 5.
[3] Neh. ii, 3.
[4] Ps. cxxxvii.
[5] Yet the experience of sporadic persecution may at least lie behind the later story of the Three Hebrew Children in Dan. iii, for until the rise of Persia ancient kings expected their subjects to worship their gods.

at the Temple was indeed impossible—they could only long for this. But they could meet together to 'remember Zion'; they could gather round such Hebrew teachers as Ezekiel and Deutero-Isaiah; they could keep the Sabbath, copy out their distinctive laws and their hereditary stories, practise circumcision and many other of their laws. They sedulously did these things. Fire either destroys or purifies, and exile was like it. Most exiled peoples perished; Israel survived, and survives. It was now that it learnt the way to survive that has served it so well through all the ages since. To return to the figure, the fire purified their faith. The exile succeeded where all the disciplines of Palestine and all the warnings of the Prophets had failed. Or rather, in exile the teachings of Deuteronomists and Prophets at last fell on good soil and yielded harvest. It was not in Palestine but in Babylon that Israel rose from the dead. The metaphor is Ezekiel's[1] and he was a Prophet of the Exile.[2]

What was the unique achievement of the Prophets of this period? To-day it is usually expressed in two words—it is said that the Prophets from Amos to Deutero-Isaiah gave Israel the doctrine of 'ethical monotheism.' The phrase is useful and accurate, but it has too theoretical a sound. The Hebrews, and least of all the Prophets, were never mere theorists. They never showed any interest in mere theory. On the contrary, every Hebrew doctrine was meant to be practised. More, so far as its exponents could secure, it *was* practised. In the instance before us,

[1] Ezek. xxxvii.

[2] cf. Jer. xxiv, where the 'good figs' are the exiles of 597 B.C. and the 'bad figs' are the people left in Palestine.

in particular, the Prophetic doctrine was provoked by the historical situation. To show this it will be well to begin with the second word, 'monotheism.'

It has already been seen that Elijah took a first small step in overpassing the limits of the old monolatry.[1] He did this when he handed on to Elisha the task of 'anointing' Hazael to be king of Aram, for this meant that Jahveh controlled the history of Aram as well as of Israel. Amos took the next step. In his first two chapters he has a series of oracles that pronounce Jahveh's judgement, not only on Northern Israel, but on Moab and Edom and Aram and so on. He confines himself here to the small peoples that ringed Palestine, but it does not seem to have occurred to him that Jahveh had nothing to do with any race but the Hebrew. In other words, strict monolatry has gone. It might be asked, however, whether Jahveh had anything to do with the nations further afield, and especially with the great empire of Assyria that was striding in conquest across the world of Israel's knowledge. It fell to Isaiah clearly and finally to answer this question. It is not easy for us to put ourselves in his place, but only if we do so can we understand his superb achievement. Assyria had conquered many a nation to the north of Judah—Hamath and Arpad, Aram and Israel and so on. And Assyria claimed to do this in the power of its god. It asserted that neither nations nor their gods—for in ancient thought the two went together—could withstand Assyria and its god. This is the claim of Assyrian inscriptions and it is born out by the Old Testament. When Sennacherib sent messengers to Jerusalem, they took this precise point—'Where are

[1] pp. 48f.

the gods of Hamath and of Arpad? Where are the gods of Sepharvaim, of Hena, and Ivvah? Have they delivered Samaria out of my hand? Who are they among all the gods of the countries, that have delivered their country out of my hand, that Jahveh should deliver Jerusalem out of my hand?' Before Assyria gods and nations were going down together. Judah was one of the smallest of these peoples, and Sennacherib had overthrown every city of Judah but one, shutting up Hezekiah, as he says in one of his famous inscriptions, in Jerusalem 'like a bird in a cage.' Only two ways were open to Isaiah and he unhesitatingly took the right one. Either Jahveh must 'go under' or he is greater than Assyria. Isaiah looked from the wall of Jahveh's last beleagured city and asserted that the seemingly omnipotent empire was nothing more than a tool of Jahveh! He is merely the 'rod of (Jahveh's) anger' and when Assyria has served Jahveh's turn, he will show it that it is nothing but a tool.[1] Nor does Isaiah stop there. He has oracles against Moab and Edom, Aram and Tyre, Egypt and Ethiopia, and every oracle takes it for granted that they are all in Jahveh's hands for him to do as he will with. It has been argued that Isaiah is not a theoretical monotheist—that he never says 'There is but one god.' He did something better than state any theoretical truth—he taught the faithful in Israel the *practise* of monotheism. For him Jahveh is the one indisputable master of mankind. As suggested already,[2] monolatry cannot last—it must either pass into polytheism or into monotheism. In a solitary instance it passed into monotheism, and in Isaiah we see it doing so.

[1] Isa. x, 5, 15. [2] p. 22.

All the Prophets that followed shared his conviction. Jeremiah and Ezekiel, for instance, have oracles that tell what Jahveh is going to do with this foreign nation and that. Zephaniah, facing the horror of the Scythian invasion, declares that this barbarian inroad is just Jahveh's 'besom of destruction.' When Nineveh's time came, Israel took no part in her overthrow, yet Nahum cried out with joy that Jahveh was at last flinging her down. When Cyrus' star rose in the further East, Deutero-Isaiah calls him, like David, 'Jahveh's anointed.'[1] Apart from Isaiah, there is no story of miracle in any of these Prophets.[2] For them Jahveh is god of history,[3] but it is of universal history. The natural deduction is that there is only one god and he is Jahveh. We reached this assertion in Deutero-Isaiah. He has two whole chapters on the theme.[4] As for other 'gods' they merely provoke his derision [5]; he jeers at man-made idols and their makers. For Jahveh has said to him 'I am the first, and I am the last; and beside me there is no god.'[6]

On another side too this Prophet marks a climax. So far we have considered history; what of Nature? What of the world of things, as well as of men? Here again the process of Israel's discovery does not follow the same line as modern logic. We begin by asking 'Who made the world?' The primitive question,

[1] Isa. xlv, 1.

[2] The chief instance in Isaiah is the Destruction of Sennacherib's army, and, if we may trust Herodotus, the cause of his retreat was an outbreak of plague in his huge, insanitary eastern camp, that is, as we should say, an historical event. The only event in Isaiah's story that *we* should call miracle is the obscure incident about the 'dial of Ahaz' (Isa. xxxviii, 8).

[3] cf. p. 48.

[4] Chaps. xliv and xlv.

[5] Isa. xl, 19f.; xliv, 12ff.

[6] Isa. xliv, 6.

if put into our speech, was rather, 'Who controls the world?' This was natural, for the practical problem of daily life is not 'How was the universe made in the beginning?' but 'How will next autumn's harvest come, if it comes at all?' Man does not begin by musing on origins but by seeking for daily bread. Israel's answer in its monolatrous days had been that the covenant god gives the covenant people a land 'flowing with milk and honey.' Similarly, in Elijah's day, it is he who sends the three rainless years of punishment, and he who thereafter calls the rain from the West.[1] This doctrine persists and develops in the Prophets.[2] Deutero-Isaiah takes the last step. It is not enough for him that Jahveh controls Nature. He bases his mighty message of encouragement to the feeble remnant of exiles in Babylon on the doctrine that their Helper is the god that *made* all things. 'Thus saith Jahveh that created the heavens; he is God; that formed the earth and made it . . . look unto me, and be ye saved, all the ends of the earth.'[3] In Deutero-Isaiah the development of the doctrine of monotheism is complete.

It will be seen that this is no otiose monotheism but a belief that the one God is always active. Whatever emperors and kings may think, He is all the time their master; He is doing His will with all mankind. Such a monotheism may be a terrifying creed. For it raises the urgent question, 'What kind of a god is

[1] 1 Kings xvii, f.

[2] e.g. Amos iv, 13; Hos. xiv, 5ff.; Isa. xxx, 23ff.; Jer. i, 5; Isa. lv, 12f.

[3] Isa. xlv, 18, 22. A concordance will show that the word 'create' is characteristic of Deutero-Isaiah and of Gen. i. The latter belongs to the next period (cf. p. 125). There is a parallel passage in Jer. x, 12ff. (repeated in li, 15ff.), but its date is doubtful.

this who holds us all the time in the hollow of His hand? Do we know anything of His character and so of His ways?' This brings us to our second semi-technical word, 'ethical.' It is not the Prophets' word. Their characteristic word has no abstract flavour. They declare that the one God is 'righteous.' They declare further that He expects men to be 'righteous,' and that the key to all His deeds is the answer to one question, 'Is this man, this class, this kingdom, this empire, practising righteousness?' It is a simple doctrine but a great one. A few illustrations will not only exhibit it but will also show what the Prophets meant by 'righteousness.'

While the two first of these Prophets, Amos and Hosea, have the same general message, there is a contrast between them. Throughout his oracles Amos sets his face like a flint; Hosea is subject to all the changes of emotion that befall a broken-hearted man. With him oracles of Jahveh's mercy mingle with oracles of judgement; with Amos it is judgement all the time. Yet Amos is hard because he is tender. He pitied the poor. All his messages to the various nations have one theme, though its illustrations vary; he says to them one by one, 'Thou hast been unjust to the poor—therefore Jahveh will judge and punish thee.' This herdsman is the champion of those who have no other champion—or rather, he declares that Jahveh is their champion. It follows that for the Prophets righteousness is a social concept, and that two of its elements are justice and mercy. For them, in contrast to many men of to-day, religion and social doctrine are one thing. They taught Israel that the 'righteous Lord loveth righteousness.'[1]

[1] Ps. xi, 7.

In the master-concept of righteousness there was a third principal element, which it is easy to illustrate from Hosea. It covers all the notions that English expresses by such words as 'truth,' 'faithfulness,' 'staunchness,' 'loyalty.' Hosea's wife was faithless.[1] Her faithlessness would show itself in many ways—in untruth of speech, in treachery of life, in disloyalty of heart. All these things Hebrew groups in one word. It is often translated 'truth,' and this may serve if it is remembered that the word means no such thing as 'scientific truth.' It means a faithfulness that permeates life—that informs the character alike of Jahveh and of a true Israelite. 'The righteous *lives* by his faithfulness.'[2]

This doctrine of righteousness, with its several ingredients, is the dominant doctrine of all the Prophets of this epoch. With them it is more—they have a passion for righteousness. Many of the most familiar of the passages from their books are just illustrations of this, but there is here no mere question of 'proof passages,' whether many or few. In these Prophets the conviction that Jahveh is righteous and demands righteousness in men is everywhere. If this were taken out of their books, there would not be a single oracle left. It is true that sometimes it is not asserted but assumed, but then men are surest of the things that they take for granted. A foundation is still a foundation even though it is only the super-structure that is described. Leaven 'leavens the whole lump' even though it is unseen. When Isaiah cries 'Cease to do evil: learn to do well; seek justice,[3] relieve the

[1] See Hos. i-iii.
[2] Hab. ii, 4.
[3] This is a better translation than 'judgement.'

oppressed, plead for the widow,'[1] he is expounding righteousness; when he catalogues the wardrobes of the mincing ladies of Jerusalem and foretells their doom, he takes it terribly for granted that Jahveh will inevitably punish those who 'merely enjoy themselves' and neglect the poor.[2] There is no passage in the Old Testament that seems more flatly to contradict the Sermon on the Mount than the prophecy of Nahum, but if we say only this we miss his emphasis. If he shouts for joy as he foresees detail by cruel detail the sack of Nineveh, it is because 'there is a god that judgeth in the earth.' For us the disappearance of the little kingdom of Judah in an epoch of great empires seems as inevitable and inconsiderable an historical event as the disappearance of Montenegro in the Great War; for Jeremiah it falls because Jahveh cannot find a single righteous man in all Jerusalem.[3] To such 'objective' historians as Herodotus or Gibbon, the rise of such an one as Cyrus or Timour or Napoleon is just a fact of history, partly explicable in 'the light of the events' of the time, partly inexplicable, for 'events' do not always generate genius; for Deutero-Isaiah Jahveh 'raises up' Cyrus to vindicate His righteousness in the saving of His faithful little flock of derelict Jews. These examples raise some of the problems that beset a belief in 'ethical monotheism,' but they also show the greatness of the Prophetic concept. It was in darkness that they struck this light, and no darkness since has quenched it. Monotheism would be an intolerable creed if the one God were capricious; if He is righteous, it is the creed to live by. To revert to the 'remnant' in Israel—under the ethical demands of the Prophets

[1] Isa. i, 16f. [2] Isa. iii, 16ff. [3] Jer. v, 1.

the evils of syncretism were banned; under monotheism, polytheism perished.

As already stated, the Prophets' doctrine of ethical monotheism took a practical form—If men do unrighteousness, Jahveh will punish them; if men do righteousness, Jahveh will bless them. There is here a doctrine of prosperity, as well as of ethics. Just as there were earlier anticipations of the doctrine of righteousness,[1] so there were of the doctrine of prosperity. It will be remembered that the old monolatous concept of Covenant included the belief that Jahveh would bless His people, if only they were faithful to him.[2] The Prophets universalized this idea. It is true that, when they were dealing with other nations beside Israel, the negative truth—that a sinful nation will perish—monopolized their attention,[3] for they believed that all the nations were wicked. This idea culminated in their doctrine of 'the Day of Jahveh.' Apparently, this phrase did not originate with them,[4] but it was they who moralized it. The Hebrews, like some other nations, had already the belief that in the future their god would win a final victory over their enemies. The Prophets adopted this idea,[5] but they made the victory a final demonstration of Jahveh's righteous judgement of the nations. It was to be a 'day' of punishment for sin—a 'day' of which all earlier victories were only a prelude. All the nations, since all were wicked, were to fall under a general doom.

Was doom to be the final fate of *Israel*? Here the opposite truth emerges. It is true that some

[1] pp. 31f. [2] pp. 18ff.
[3] Or almost monopolized it, see below, pp. 75, 76f.
[4] Amos v, 18.
[5] They often use the word 'day' in this sense.

Prophets, notably Amos, seem to expect nothing but punishment for Israel, as for the other peoples.[1] He tells his fellow-Hebrews, who expect that the 'Day of Jahveh' will give Israel final victory, that for them, as for other nations, 'the Day of Jahveh is darkness and not light,' for they too have sinned. But with some of the Prophets there is a better hope for Jahveh's people. They expect that the ordeal of punishment will lead them to 'return unto Jahveh'—or at least will lead a 'remnant' of them to do so—and when they have turned to righteousness, Jahveh will send them triumph and prosperity. 'I will heal their backslidings, I will love them freely' says Hosea.[2] 'Thine ears,' says Isaiah, 'shall hear a word behind thee, saying, "This is the way, walk thee in it" . . . and he shall give rain . . . and bread . . . and there shall be upon every lofty mountain and upon every high hill, rivers and streams of waters, in the day of the great slaughter . . . in the day that Jahveh bindeth up the hurt of his people and healeth the stroke of their wound.'[3] Jeremiah taught persistently that Jahveh would send His people into captivity, but he added that He would restore them—'Thus saith the Lord, Behold, I will turn again the captivity of Jacob's tents, and have compassion on his dwelling-places . . . and I will punish all that oppress them . . . and ye shall be my people, and I will be your God.'[4] While Ezekiel spends many oracles upon the denunciations of wicked Israel, he ends his book with a picture of a restored Zion, lying happily about a restored Temple. Deutero-Isaiah's chief calling is to sing of a Return.

[1] Amos ix, 11-15, is almost certainly a later fragment, for it represents Judah as fallen, and this did not happen for a century and a half after Amos.

[2] Hos. xiv, 4. [3] Isa. xxx, 19-26. [4] Jer. xxx, 16-22.

Since monarchy was the universal form of rule in the world, it was natural that the Prophets should think of this halcyon future as a kingdom. This brings us to the subject of what is called 'Messianic prophecy.'[1] Sometimes the figure of the king is subordinate, at others it is prominent. A quotation from Isaiah's oracles may be given to illustrate each attitude. 'Behold a king shall reign in righteousness, and princes shall rule in justice'—so he begins one of his messages of hope, but after this first verse nothing more is said of the king.[2] The second passage is still more familiar—'For unto us a child is born, unto us a son is given; and the government shall be upon his shoulder: and his name shall be called Wonderful Counsellor, Mighty God, Everlasting Father, Prince of Peace. Of the increase of his government and of peace there shall be no end, upon the throne of David, and upon his kingdom, to establish it, and to uphold it with justice and with righteousness from henceforth even for ever. The zeal of the Lord of Hosts shall perform this.'[3] While this kind of oracle has nowhere many instances, the chief are in Isaiah.

The last quotation illustrates two further phenomena. The Prophets sometimes at least seem to expect the Kingdom of Jahveh's righteousness soon—and this, though again and again it is delayed. Here they were mistaken. Secondly, in their concept of prosperity, peace is an element. Faced as they were with empires whose strength was war, it would not have been remarkable if they had foretold a future of mere conquest for Israel. They do expect that Jahveh

[1] Though the word 'Messiah,' or Anointed (king), does not occur in these Prophets till Isa. xlv, 1, and then of Cyrus.

[2] Isa. xxxii, 1-8.

[3] Isa. ix, 6f.

will win a great victory, but this is a means, not an end. The end is peace. The frequent parable of the Shepherd King illustrates this, for a shepherd is a man of peace. 'I will make with them a covenant of peace, and will cause evil beasts to cease out of the land: and they shall dwell securely in the wilderness, and sleep in the woods . . . and ye my sheep, the sheep of my pasture, are men, and I am your God, saith the Lord Jahveh.'[1] Is there any picture of peace to surpass this—that it is safe for a sheep to sleep in a wilderness?

Three great prophecies of peace, included in the Book of Isaiah, may be named here.[2] There is difference of opinion about their date—not so much because they promise peace as because they expect the conversion of the nations. The problem cannot be discussed here, but, whenever the great oracle of the first paragraph of the Eleventh Chapter of Isaiah was placed next to the last of the Tenth, a genius did it, for the two oracles place side by side two ideals—the ideal of a warlike empire, typified by Assyria, and the ideal of a world at peace, typified by the reign of a 'Shoot out of the stump of Jesse.' Similarly, the first of these oracles foretells a League of Nations. This is no mere modern idea. The novelty to-day is the concept of a League of Nations that has no necessary connexion with God.

Twice about this time it seemed for a moment as though this belief in Jahveh's deliverance of a righteous Israel were being vindicated. The first was when Jahveh thrust back Sennacherib from Jerusalem;

[1] Ezek. xxxiv, 25-31.

[2] Isa. ii, 2-4; xi, 1-9; xix, 18-25. The first of these is repeated in Mic. iv, 1-4. The last may be a combination of two or three short oracles.

the second when He 'raised up' Cyrus to 'perform all his will' in the restoration of the faithful remnant. In both cases fulfilment fell far short of expectation. Yet both instances give the right perspective to the Prophetic doctrine of prosperity. Sometimes to-day we are told that the Prophets told Israel to be righteous *in order to* prosper. In other words, we are told that they did not love righteousness for its own sake. This is quite to mistake their approach to the subject of prosperity. For them the ruling concept is that Jahveh Himself is righteous—and therefore, because of His own character, He must give prosperity to the righteous. To do otherwise would be to deny Himself. This is peculiarly clear in Deutero-Isaiah. For him the two terms 'righteousness' and 'salvation' go together, almost as a single concept.[1] Jahveh is righteous; therefore He must save the righteous—for the Prophets this is the beginning and end of the matter.

But is Israel alone to be saved? Is it only in this one people that there is a righteous 'remnant'? This question inevitably arises for us when we think over the Prophets' doctrine of Prosperity, but, unless the three oracles in Isaiah named above,[2] belong to Isaiah, no Prophet faces it before the Exile. As already seen, for the Prophets other nations are simply wicked, and there was practical ground for this axiom. But the idea that the nations may turn to Jahveh and so survive and flourish emerges certainly in the so-called 'Servant Songs' of Deutero-Isaiah.[3] 'And he said unto me, Thou art my servant, Israel, in whom I will be glorified. . . . It is too light a thing

[1] Isa. li, 4-8; lvi, 1. [2] p. 75.
[3] Isa. xlii, 1-7; xlix, 1-6; l, 4-9; lii, 13-liii, 12.

that thou shouldst be my servant to raise up the tribes of Jacob, and to restore the preserved of Israel: I will also give thee to be a light to the Gentiles, that my salvation may be unto the end of the earth.'[1] The greatest of the Servant Songs[2] is probably best interpreted in the same sense. Its theme is that Israel, or the godly remnant in Israel, is vicariously suffering to redeem mankind. It is the other nations who cry of the Servant of Jahveh, 'Surely he hath borne our griefs and carried our sorrows . . . He was wounded for our transgressions . . . with his stripes we are healed.'[3] For this nameless preacher of an obscure fragment of an exiled race Jahveh is the redeemer of all nations. Why do the righteous suffer? We shall find this question clamant in the next period.[4] Deutero-Isaiah already gives the noblest reply—Jahveh's 'righteous servant' suffers for others. It is a final illustration of the truth that man is corporate or societary, and that therefore men and nations can harm or help, ruin or save, each other.

Yet men are individual as well as societary, and this too has a leading illustration a little earlier in this period. 'The fathers have eaten sour grapes and the children's teeth are set on edge.' This proverb occurs both in Jeremiah and Ezekiel. There was a time when if a Hebrew had heard it, he would have said, 'Yes, of course, why not?' For in early days a man's family were part of his possession and men thought it right, for instance, that Achan's

[1] Isa. xlix, 3, 6.
[2] Isa. lii, 13-liii, 12.
[3] The various expositions of this great oracle will be found in the commentaries. The above seems the right one to the writer. It involves the change of the phrase 'my people' in ver. 8 into 'the peoples,' but it seems best to suit the whole passage.
[4] pp. 104ff.

family should perish with him for his sin.[1] But it was quoted by Jeremiah and Ezekiel's hearers as an objection to the message of Jahveh's righteousness. They both replied that the proverb was false—that Jahveh would deal with every man according to his own deeds.[2] Sometimes this is rather inaccurately interpreted to mean that they 'discovered the individual.' The truth rather is that people generally had done this,[3] and therefore claimed that in punishing the men of one generation for the sins of earlier generations Jahveh is not righteous. The Prophets reply that He will deal with men *one by one*. It is true that they also declare that Jahveh will punish Israel as a unrighteous *nation*, and that they do not logically harmonize the two assertions. No one has ever yet harmonized them, for this is only one example of the difficulties that attend the fact that men are by nature both corporate and individual, and to harmonize these two phenomena has always defeated the wit of man. None the less the two Prophets do not falter. Difficulties or no difficulties, they are sure that Jahveh is righteous and that therefore He will judge every man by his own deeds. In modern phrase they say 'Yes, you are right, men are individuals; they ought not therefore to suffer because their fathers have sinned; Jahveh will see to it that they don't.' In yet other modern words, they declare that every single man 'has worth for God.'[4] This is for

[1] Josh. vii, 24f. [2] Jer. xxxi, 29f.; Ezek. xviii.

[3] I have traced the stages in *The Bible Doctrine of Society*. See 'Individualism' in its index.

[4] It ensues that the Prophets denounce human sacrifice (e.g., Jer. xix, 5). Earlier it had been possible in Hebraism (Jud. xi, 39), though not obligatory (Gen. xxii, 12f.). It was apparently a leading element in the worship of Moloch (e.g., 2 Kings xxiii, 10) whose cult kept on reappearing, at least under evil kings.

religious men the ultimate account of 'individuality' or 'personality.' It adds another item to the doctrine of righteousness.

But Jeremiah—and after him Ezekiel, though less distinctly—took a further step. By its very nature righteousness is a personal quality. A nation can only be righteous in a derivative sense—it can only be righteous if the men that compose it are righteous. In reality all the appeals of all the Prophets for righteousness were made to individuals, though before Jeremiah they hardly seem to have thought this out. In his own way he did so. The greatest of his oracles is the oracle of the 'covenant of the heart.'[1] The day, he says, is to come when Israel's old national—and therefore external, and therefore insufficient—covenant shall be superseded. Instead, every man shall know and obey Jahveh for himself—and so there shall be a righteous people. 'I will put my law in their inward parts, and in their heart will I write it; and (so) I will be their God and they shall be my people.' From the doctrine of the righteous character of God the Prophets deduce that His every individual worshipper ought to be righteous through and through. Righteousness is a principle, and principle belongs primarily to inward motive and only secondarily to outward act.

The Prophets, then, did justice to one of the three elements in religion, the ethical. What of the other two, the ritual and the spiritual? In the past it has often been supposed that their chief message was the denunciation of mere ritual, and it is true that this bulks largely in their oracles. In particular, they relentlessly denounced image worship. But their chief contribution to religion is not negative but positive—

[1] Jer. xxxi, 31ff., cf. Ezek. xxxvi, 26f.

not the denial of value to ritual but the assertion of the supreme value of righteousness. Yet this positive involved a negative, and this showed itself in the realm of ritual. First, they denounce idolatry—that is, the use of images in worship. Here again, it may be possible to argue theoretically that the use of images need not conflict with ethical monotheism, but the Prophets take practical ground. In the experience of Israel, as in the experience of nations generally, the use of images contradicted both ethics and monotheism. The facts have already been described in the account of syncretism in the last chapter.[1] To take again the most glaring instance—alongside the Baal there went the image of Ashtart, and with this there went sexual worship and the notion that there was more than one god—a female alongside a male. The Prophets, therefore, are intolerant of the image, for its use contradicted their message in both its parts. Here again Isaiah may stand for all—'There shall be a Day of Jahveh of Hosts upon all that is proud and haughty . . . and Jahveh alone shall be exalted in that day. And the idols shall utterly pass away . . . In that day a man shall cast away his idols of silver, and his idols of gold, which they made for him to worship, to the moles and to the bats . . . from before the terror of Jahveh, and from the glory of his majesty, when he ariseth to shake mightily the earth.'[2] Here is the doom of the syncretism that had infected Israel for centuries.

But what of the rest of ritual? There are some passages which, taken alone, seem to say that the Prophets, apart from Ezekiel,[3] counted it *all* sinful

[1] pp. 36ff. [2] Isa. ii, 12-22. [3] See p. 88.

and declared for a religion without ritual.[1] There are others that seem to assume, more or less clearly, that they took it for granted that in the pure worship of the future ritual would have a place.[2] The subject cannot be discussed here, but to me it seems that the passages that seem to cry out upon all ritual are instances of the kind of hyperbole that is common with earnest preachers, and that it is very unlikely that practical men like the Prophets should envisage such an unexampled phenomenon as a worship without ritual. In particular it seems to me unlikely that Isaiah, whose Call seems to have occurred in the Temple,[3] and who declared in the hour of Sennacherib's terror that Jerusalem, the city of the Temple, should not fall, would or could have dreamed of a future when there should be nothing but what is called a 'purely spiritual' worship. If the Prophets did so dream, they dreamed of the impossible, for, whatever may be the facts in individual worship, no corporate worship can forego ritual of some sort. Even the early Quakers, when they kept their hats on in worship, were making a ritual protest against ritual! But, whatever be the truth in this dispute about the Prophets, it is at least certain that they passionately denounced the idea that mere ritual can be true worship. Perhaps the best known passage is Isaiah's,[4] but there is a famous one in Micah too.[5] In it he declares that even for a man to sacrifice his son, a piece of ritual still practised[6] under the idea that a god *must* hear

[1] e.g. Amos v, 21ff., Isa. i, 10-17, Mic. vi, 6-8.

[2] e.g. Isa. xxxiii, 20; Jer. xxxiii, 11; Hab. ii, 20. Some other passages, especially Jer. xvii, 19-27 (an oracle in defence of the Sabbath, which, of course, is a piece of ritual), are assigned by many experts to a later date.

[3] Isa. vi, 1ff.

[4] Isa. i, 10-17.

[5] Mic. vi, 6-8.

[6] Jer. vii, 31.

when he is offered *this*,[1] is useless. Or we may watch Jeremiah standing 'in the gate of Jahveh's house' and declaring to the many thronging worshippers that it is of no use to say 'This is Jahveh's Temple, This is Jahveh's Temple.' Let them go to the deserted site of Shiloh and see what Jahveh did to His shrine there, and learn that it is no use to 'come and stand before (him) in this house' and say 'We are safe,' when they 'steal, murder, and commit adultery, and swear falsely . . . and walk after other gods.'[2] Jahveh will not tolerate ritual without righteousness.

The achievement of the Prophets here may be put in various ways. They clearly distinguished between ritual and ethics. They put ritual in its proper subordinate place in religion. They gave ethics a permanent place at the core of religion. To us these things are commonplaces, but it was the Prophets who made them so. To get the right perspective of their triumph we need to recall a great part of the history of all religion. At first, both in Israel and elsewhere, ritual and ethics lay side by side undifferentiated.[3] With progressive races, however, there came a time when these were distinguished. When this happened, usually ethics and religion parted company and went their several ways. There were sometimes more or less adequate protests, as with Zoroaster, but these were unsuccessful. Later Zoroastrianism fell into little but ritual. Originally both Confucianism and Buddhism taught an ethic that was not organically related to current religion. It is only possible for modern exponents of Hinduism to rescue its gods from immoralities by a desperate attempt to symbolize their stories. In Greece and Rome ethics and religion

[1] cf. 2 Kings iii, 27. [2] Jer. vii, 1-15. [3] cf. pp. 31f.

fell so far apart that men went seeking true religion in many strange places. Only in Israel were there men who effectively 'saved the situation.' First in a single small people, and then through Christianity in the world at large, the Prophets made 'current coin' of the belief that without ethics there can be no true worship. Elsewhere what we call 'superstition'—the idea that the gods were satisfied if they were worshipped with the ritual that they chose—was universal in popular religion. The Prophets have taught us that true religion demands that a man shall 'do justly, love mercy and walk humbly with (his) God.'[1]

Before asking what contribution the Prophets made to the third element in religion, the spiritual, it will be well to turn to the Deuteronomists. It will be remembered that these men were active from the days of Josiah, or even Hezekiah,[2] till the middle of the Exile. This means that the period of their literary activity fell after the days of Amos, Hosea and Isaiah, and during the days of Jeremiah and Ezekiel. It is necessary therefore to ask briefly how far they agreed with the message of the Prophets and how far they differed from it.

The Deuteronomists, like the Prophets, were monotheists. The text usually quoted has long been the watchword of Jewish monotheism—'Hear, O Israel: Jahveh our God is one Jahveh.'[3] To us the phrase seems a rather curious one, and the margin of the Revised Version shows how variously it may be rendered into English. Perhaps its form is best explained from the background of syncretism. In the days of Manasseh, as earlier, there were multitudes

[1] Mic. vi, 8. [2] pp. 53ff. [3] Deut. vi, 4.

of local sanctuaries in Israel, and, especially when we remember that for the Canaanites each Baal, at each local sanctuary, was a different Baal, we can see that it would be easy for the Hebrew-Canaanite race to think that there were many Jahvehs. If this is so, the famous text is a declaration of monotheism as over against syncretism. Another text needs no such explication of the context—'Jahveh, he is God in heaven above and upon the earth beneath: there is none else.'[1] This chapter is probably one of the latest of Deuteronomic products, but we are here taking the final findings of this school. The same passage shows that the Deuteronomists were in vehement agreement with the Prophetic denunciation of idols—'Take heed unto yourselves, lest ye forget the convenant of Jahveh your God, which he made with you, and make you a graven image in the form of anything which Jahveh thy God hath forbidden thee. For Jahveh thy God is a devouring fire, a jealous God.'[2] Again, the Deuteronomists, like the Prophets, teach that Jahveh is master both of nations and Nature, and that He blesses those who obey Him and punishes those who disobey. As already seen[3] their whole work is just a great sermon on this text.

Some other points of likeness will appear below. Of differences three are principal. The first, springs from the fact that there is so large an element of law in the Book of Deuteronomy.[4] Like all laws, in the strict sense of the term, the laws of Israel deal with outward act rather than inward motive. Again, they presuppose a given historical situation and therefore cannot be applied *verbatim* to other historical situa-

[1] Deut. iv, 39.
[2] Deut. iv, 23f.
[3] pp.. 55f.
[4] Chaps. xii-xxvi.

tions. For instance, a number of Deuteronomic laws are laws about bondmen, and about such bondmen as were found in Hebrew villages. In lands where there is no slavery, they do not run. Yet it is possible to overrate the importance of this feature of the work of the Deuteronomists. For they are not busy merely with law in the strict sense. For them law is 'torah' or teaching, and there are many passages, both in Deuteronomy itself and in the Deuteronomic redaction of other books that are not legal, even in form, but that do teach.[1] Even in the midst of a series of laws, in the strict sense of the term, they can cry out, for instance, 'Righteousness, righteousness shalt thou follow.'[2] And it is in Deuteronomy that we meet the great assertion of the final motive of religious men—'Thou shalt love Jahveh thy God with all thine heart, and with all thy soul, and with all thy might.'[3] The truth is that in the writings of this school we see the impact of the great Prophetic principle of Righteousness on law and on the priesthood that was the guardian of law. As already seen,[4] there was an ethical element in earlier Hebrew law—an ethical element that especially showed itself in care for the poor. The Prophets had elucidated the principle that all the while underlay such precepts. Such elucidation is rare and precious in history. The Prophets, of course, applied the principle to many of the details of the life around them, but the principle itself is as versatile and permanent as human life and is timeless. Under its influence the Deuteronomists enlarged the old laws and made new ones, applying the principle to the details of their own day.

[1] e.g. Deut. iv; vi; xxviii; 1 Kings viii, 23-61; xvii, 7-23.
[2] Deut. xvi, 20. [3] Deut. vi, 5. [4] pp. 31ff.

Consequently, while the teaching of the Prophets is timeless, the *distinctive* teaching of the Deuteronomists belongs to a given time. They give a great example to later generations of the practical application of Righteousness to the detail of everyday life. Their laws have often been called 'humanitarian,' but they are humanitarian in the name of God. It will be well if we apply the great principle as effectively to the details of the life of our time.

The other difference between the Deuteronomists and the Prophets (again apart from Ezekiel[1]) is more serious. No one can review the work of the Deuteronomic redactors without noticing their absorbing interest in the Temple. When they reach the story of Solomon they spend themselves on a description of the new shrine that he built for Jahveh. The long and eloquent prayer that they put into his mouth at its dedication[2] is a good example of their constant attitude. Again, alike in the stories of Jehoiada, of Hezekiah and Hilkiah, their love of the Temple flames out. For them the typical sin is 'the sin of Jeroboam, the son of Nebat,' and this centred in his setting up of two shrines whose eminence competed with the Temple's. But for them, at least in their latest phase,[3] the Temple is not merely Jahveh's chief shrine; it is His only shrine. They vehemently denounce not only Jeroboam's two great sanctuaries at Bethel and Dan, but all the local 'high places.' For them these are Canaanite shrines and therefore sinful. In view of the syncretism that persistently beset the 'high places,' it is easy to understand the

[1] pp. 80, 88. [2] 1 Kings viii, 23-61.
[3] Deut. xii, 5-14. The Hebrew of the parallel passages does not, in the opinion of some scholars, certainly imply a 'single sanctuary.'

Deuteronomists animus against them. These men, it seems clear, held that from the days when the Temple was built onwards, Jahveh ought to have been worshipped there and nowhere else. According to the record Hezekiah tried to secure this; it was a chief item in Josiah's reforms.[1] The practical basis of this creed is easy to discern—the Temple was under the immediate eye of the king, and there a king who was loyal to Jahveh could successfully order the *cultus* aright. For a moment under Josiah this was done, but what when the king was bad? The successors of Josiah gave the inevitable answer. With them the evils of Manasseh returned. None the less the Deuteronomists still treasured their ideal of a 'single sanctuary' under a faithful king. For them the 'law of the single sanctuary' was the pivot of religion. After the Exile they triumphed. As we shall see, in the sequel Israel accepted and practised this creed. Orthodox Judaism believes to this day that sacrifice may be rightly offered at just one spot in the wide world.

The teaching of the Deuteronomists here clashes with that of the Prophets. For a belief in the Temple means a belief in the extreme importance of right ritual. It was for the practice of this that the Temple existed. Consequently we find in the Book of Deuteronomy many commands about sacrifices and feasts and priests. Further, there is no distinction made between these and commands that involve ethics. For the Deuteronomists, for instance, it is just as important that a man should keep the rota of Feasts as that he should do justice without 'respect of persons.' The two lie side by side, quite

[1] 2 Kings xviii, 4, 22; xxii, 8, 15.

undifferentiated, in the Sixteenth Chapter. Here is the chief defect of the Deuteronomists, and here too they were the fathers of the next age.

At this point one Prophet goes with the Deuteronomists. Ezekiel, like Jeremiah, was of priestly family, but, unlike Jeremiah, he had the heart of a priest—he loved ritual. Like the other Prophets he has a passion for Righteousness, but unlike them he adds ritual to Righteousness. At the end of his book he gives nine chapters[1] to a description of the Palestine that is to be, and in this account he spends himself chiefly on the future city, and in the city on the future Temple. It is uncertain how far he builds upon the ritual of the old Temple that lay in ruins, but it is certain that for him an ideal ritual is the crown of hope. Again, like the Deuteronomists he does not draw the line clearly between ethics and ritual. For instance, for him the encroachment of the burial ground of the kings of David's house on the area of the Temple court is as great an outrage as injustice itself.[2] He is a great symbolist, and it is doubtful how far he expected that his dreams could find literal fulfilment, for many symbolists pass carelessly across the boundaries that divide the literal from the symbolic, but it is certain that for him a right ritual was the inevitable complement of righteousness. Unlike the other Prophets he makes frequent use of the great ritual word 'holy.' As Prophet he belongs to this period, as priest he anticipates the next.

The third difference between the Prophets and Deuteronomists has often been summed in misleading phrases. It has been said that it is a question 'of prophet against priest,' or 'of the "living voice"

[1] Ezek. xl-xlviii. [2] Ezek. xliii, 7-9.

against "dead tradition,"' or 'of "immediate revelation" against Canon.' These phrases simplify overmuch. It is true that, while there had been collections of written laws earlier in Israel, Josiah's acceptance of 'the Book of the Law' did mark an epoch. For the first time a Canon—that is, a collection of authoritative books—takes a dominant place in Hebraism, a place that it has never since lost. Yet the Canon does not supersede the 'living voice.' Josiah himself does not accept Hilkiah's book till he has consulted the 'living voice' of Huldah the prophetess.[1] Again, the Book of Deuteronomy itself teaches that Moses, himself the first Prophet, declared that Jahveh would raise up a succession of Prophets like him for the guidance of Israel.[2] Further, a Canon derives ultimately from a 'living voice' or 'voices.' It records the revelations of men who once lived. On the other hand, the Prophets do not denounce the Law. Once or twice, indeed, they seem to appeal to it, and it is at least possible that Jeremiah for a while supported Josiah and Hilkiah in their advocacy of the Book of the Law.[3] For the most part they let the subject alone—yet they show no trace of the idea that their preaching is novel. On the contrary they assume that Israel has from of old been the people of Jahveh. In reality there is here a likeness with a difference within it. As seen above,[4] there are traces in early Israel of various ways of learning the will of Israel's god—of such ways as omen and lot, which other peoples used. These are now gone. It is agreed now that Jahveh makes His will known through selected men, called 'prophets.' But in the main

[1] 2 Kings xxii, 12ff.
[2] Deut. xviii, 15ff.
[3] This is one account of Jer. xi, 1-8.
[4] pp. 26ff.

the priests discover this will in the records of men of the past, the Prophets hear the voice of Jahveh for themselves. In both cases, however, Jahveh makes His will known to selected men, and these men tell it to the people at large. Revelation is through 'men of God.'

Both in the appeal to a Prophet and to a Canon there are advantages and disadvantages. These cannot be exhaustively examined here, though one or two will emerge in the discussion. In passing it may be noted that all the great religions, in varying ways and degrees, use both appeals. The immediately pertinent question is 'If men learn the will of God through certain men, how are they to know which men these are? How can they recognize a "man of God"?'

When the appeal is to men of the past the usual answer is 'Our fathers recognized this man and that as a "man of God" and so do we.' This is not a foolish answer, for in many things we accept the findings of our fathers. But it throws us back on another question—'Why did they accept this man and that as "men of God"?' To this there is no answer unless we believe that there is something in man that does rightly recognize a 'word' that comes from God. There was a man called Moses who believed that Jahveh spoke to him, and there were people who thought so too; since his day the line of those who believe this has never ceased; on the contrary, their number has grown and grown. Beyond this we cannot go. It does not imply the infallibility of Moses, though it does imply his authority. However illogical it may be, men do and must accept the authority of fallible guides. We accept the authority, for instance, of lawyers, doctors and engineers, each in his own realm, without reckoning any of them infallible. It is the same in religion. Multitudes believe that Francis, or Luther, or Wesley, was a 'man of God' without asserting his infallibility. The idea that God spoke to the mind of some man lies behind all Canons.

If we turn from the Deuteronomists to the Prophets the question takes another form. *We* accept the authority of the Prophets in part because of tradition—in part because 'our fathers have told us'—and in part because when we read them our own consciousness vindicates our fathers' judgement. But there can be no appeal to the verdict of the past when the man who claims to declare the will of God is a contemporary. We have seen above that in early Israel the usually recognized sign that a man was a Prophet was something like ecstasy.[1] But as early as the days of Ahab two men, both accredited by such phenomena, might contradict each other.[2] Which gave the true message? There is evidence both in Deuteronomy[3] and in the Prophetic books themselves[4] that in the period now in hand there were many 'false prophets.' In Jeremiah's time, in particular, they infested Jerusalem—'A wonderful and horrible thing is come to pass in the land; the prophets prophesy falsely, and the priests bear rule by their means; and my people love to have it so; and what will ye do in the end thereof?'[5] How were the people to know which were true and which were false?

1 pp. 28f.
2 1 Kings xxii, 1-28.
3 Deut. xviii, 20-22.
4 e.g. Mic. ii, 11; Jer. xxiii, 9-40; xxix, 21-32; Ezek. xiii.
5 Jer. v, 30f.

The appeal to such tokens as ecstasy and vision failed, for all claimants to prophecy had them.[1] Deuteronomy proposed to solve the difficulty by appealing to a prophet's success in foretelling the future,[2] and there were instances where this appeal could be made,[3] but clearly it would not always serve, for prophetic messages did not always foretell the future and in any case a hearer would have to wait for the future for proof, while such an anxious inquirer as king Zedekiah needed guidance at once.[4] In effect the true Prophet was distinguishable from the false by his message. He himself was conscious that Jahveh had spoken to him, and some hearers thought so too. Once more the importance of the 'godly remnant' appears. For them the true Prophet had an authentic message because of its nature. In course of time others came to agree with them, till at last, when this period was over and the Prophets were, like Moses, men of the past, all Israel came to agree with them, and so their oracles passed into the Canon. The true basis of the belief that a Prophet was 'inspired,' if that ambiguous word is to be used, was a man's own conviction, and the conviction of a group of his hearers, that God had spoken to him, and through him to them. This is what is meant by 'the Prophetic consciousness.'

It follows that there was now a new definition of a prophet, or rather than an idea that had all the while underlain the old conviction that God spoke through such men as Moses and Nathan and Elijah, grew clear.

[1] e.g. Amos vii, 12, 16; Jer. xxiii, 25, 32; Ezek. xx, 46. The term 'drop' or 'drip' seems to mean that prophets foamed at the mouth in ecstasy.

[2] Deut. xviii, 21f.

[3] e.g. Jer. xxviii.

[4] e.g. Jer. xxi.

The outward phenomena of prophecy no longer held the field. They sank into the background. A Prophet now is a man who tells other men the truth about the will of God.

So we come to the third element in religion, the spiritual. In the Prophets it is heir to the concept of the numinous.[1] For them Jahveh is still awe-ful and 'other.'[2] No one can read the story of Isaiah's Call without feeling this. No one, again, can take the trouble to make out what Ezekiel's first vision is, without being aware that 'the appearance of the likeness of the glory of Jahveh'[3] is numinous. Jeremiah, again, is strangely familiar with Jahveh; again and again we overhear them in conversation; yet all the while Jeremiah knows that he is held to his terrible task by the unseen God who has him in His irresistible grasp. Yet with the sense of the numinous there goes the conviction that Jahveh has spoken and the Prophet has heard. There is fellowship between them—a fellowship not of the Prophet's initiative but of Jahveh's. Jeremiah's deep anticipation of the future type of man had its anticipation in his own experience. Jahveh had 'put his law in (his) inward parts, and in (his) heart he (had) written it.'[4] The word 'spirit' is not common in this period till Ezekiel, probably because it was part of the lingo of the false prophets,[5] but it is the right word for us. A Prophet was a man who told the truth about the

[1] pp. 24f.

[2] Not, however, 'wholly other' either in the sense of 'wholly separate' or of 'wholly different,' for the word 'spiritual' implies fellowship, and there can be no fellowship, as psychology shows, between two beings who are wholly separate or wholly different.

[3] Ezek. i, 28.

[4] Jer. xxxi, 33.

[5] cf. 1 Kings xxii, 28.

will of the righteous and merciful God, for to him there had been given the Spirit of God. So he had conscious fellowship with the Most High. This is the spiritual element in religion—at once its climax and its core.[1]

[1] In Deuteronomy, too, there is the numinous element, for instance, in its account of the theophany at Horeb (Deut. iv, 1-40), and in its emphasis on the 'fear' that is due to Jahveh, but it has only one or two hints of the sublimation of the numinous in the spiritual (e.g. Deut. xxx, 11-14).

CHAPTER III

CONSERVATION—THE TEMPLE AND THE CANON

THIS chapter covers a period of six hundred years (538 B.C.—A.D. 70.). It falls readily into two parts—the Persian and the Hellenistic. Of these the first fills two centuries (538-331 B.C.), and the second four (331 B.C.—A.D. 70), the dividing point being the year that Alexander came into Palestine. It is now proper to use the term 'Jew' as an alternative for 'Hebrew,' for the main mass of Israelites who were still faithful to their own God ran back historically to the Kingdom of Judah, not the Kingdom of the North. Of the general history of the world in which they lived we have now fairly extensive accounts, for with Herodotus there begins the period when men studied and wrote history for its own sake. Yet these accounts are almost wholly Gentile. Neither now, nor at any other period, did the Hebrew love history merely because it is history. Even Josephus is not a true exception. His records of much of this period, though often inaccurate, are invaluable—yet he wrote, not for love of history, but to commend his people to Gentiles. On the other hand, apart from history there is a large Hebrew literature for the period. It is very various, for it includes Prophecy,[1] Law,[2]

[1] Haggai; Zechariah i-viii; Isaiah lvi-lxvi; Obadiah; Malachi.
[2] The Priestly Document (P) in the Pentateuch.

Psalms, the so-called 'Wisdom' Literature,[1] Fiction,[2] and Apocalypses.[3] Yet while the literature is so various, almost all its books have one subject—'God's Past, Present and Future Deliverances of Israel.' This will be illustrated once and again below. There are also bits of history within the Canon.[4] On a wide exposition, the books of the New Testament may also be included, for they give much valuable evidence about Israel in the first Christian century.

From the point of view of the Jew there was a great contrast politically between the Persian and Hellenistic periods. For the student of European history the mention of Persia suggests war, with the stories of Marathon, Thermopylæ, and so on. But to the Jew, whether he dwelt in Jerusalem, Mesopotamia or Egypt, the war on the Western frontiers of the Empire would seem as remote and as insignificant for him personally as the English war, say, in the Soudan seemed to an average Welshman. For the Jew the two centuries of Persian rule were a time of almost unbroken peace.[5] On the other hand, the four hundred years that followed were just a series of wars, punctuated by brief intervals of uncertain peace. First there were the conquests of Alexander and the quarrels among his generals for the reversion of his empire. Then Antioch and

[1] Proverbs, Job, Book of Wisdom, Sirach (Ecclesiasticus), and the writings of Philo.

[2] Esther, Jonah, Daniel i, iii-vi, Tobit, Judith, &c.

[3] Joel; Isaiah xxiv-xxvii; Zechariah ix-xiv; Daniel ii, vii-xii; Second Esdras; Book of Enoch; Testimonies of the Twelve Patriarchs, &c., &c.

[4] Ezra-Nehemiah (one book in the Hebrew) and, in the Greek Canon, First Maccabees.

[5] It is true that there might be local strife within the Empire, for otherwise Nehemiah would not have been so eager to build the walls of Jerusalem, but there is no evidence that these were needed in the Persian period.

Alexandria, the one under the Seleucids and the other under the Ptolemies, fought for the possession of Palestine. Next the Jews rose against Antiochus Epiphanes when he tried to abolish their distinctive worship, and out of the sanguinary struggle there emerged the independent state of the Maccabees. Then the Jews fell miserably out among themselves, until, after a half century of discord, the Romans under Pompey annexed the country. There followed the civil wars of the Romans—Pompey against Julius Cæsar, Brutus and Cassius against Anthony and Octavian, Anthony against Octavian—all throwing into confusion the Eastern Provinces. Meanwhile the Parthian Empire had arisen on the ruins of the eastern half of the Seleucid realm. Against them the Romans suffered one of the greatest of their reverses under Crassus. In Palestine Herod succeeded to the Maccabees. He had to begin his reign by expelling the Parthians from Jerusalem itself. Thereafter he kept peace with the world outside, but both he and the succeeding rulers of his house were all hated by the Jews, who were turbulently unwilling to submit either to a Herod or the Roman. With the reign of Augustus peace at last befell the Roman world at large, but not Palestine. There sedition and rebellion still seethed.[1] Sometimes Rome put Judea under Procurators, sometimes under some Herodian princeling, but neither experiment succeeded. In this one small bit of her world she failed to impose tranquillity. After a while she was again divided against herself, and the Jews seized the opportunity and rose in fierce rebellion. After an almost incredible resistance Jerusalem fell and the Temple

[1] cf. Luke xiii, 1; Acts v, 36f.

perished.[1] After the two centuries of Persian Peace there fell four hundred years of reiterating confusion and war.

The period was almost fatal to nationality. As it progressed such nations as the Aramæan, the Moabite and the Ammonite perished in the East, and Athens, Sparta and Sicily farther West. The several parts into which Alexander's empire fell at his death never became real nations. Rome itself, as has often been shown, secured its rule, not merely by the triumphs of its armies, but because the great City was wise enough to extend her citizenship little by little until men of many races could all call themselves 'Romans.' There is an instance in a certain Jew named Saul, who was a native of Tarsus, a Greek city of Asia Minor. Yet Saul belonged also to the one exception. Forlorn, weakened, broken, Israel persisted in being a nation. Her one centre was a second-rate city in the highlands of little Palestine. The rest of her children were scattered, seemingly impotent, in alien lands—first in Egypt and the Mesopotamian plain, later also in Syria, Asia Minor, Greece and Italy. Yet she survived. Alone in all the world from the Euphrates to the Atlantic she never really submitted. It was in this period that the Jew fully learnt the secret by which he persists to this day.

There is no doubt where the secret lay. It lay in the religion of the Jew. Here too he was the great exception. In religion at large, four tendencies may be discerned, particularly in the Hellenistic period. First, national religions perished with the nations

[1] This brings us to the limit of our period at A.D. 70, but, after another interval of sullen half-submission, a last Jewish revolt burst suddenly out under Bar-Cochba, and the Roman made a full end. With A.D. 135 Israel ceased to exist politically.

that practised them and a universal syncretism ensued. Here the two centuries of Persian dominion were chiefly preparatory, for the Persians seem to have left subject races to worship as they liked. For instance, they let the Babylonians, the Egyptians and the Jews follow their own faiths. Yet there was continual coming and going within their empire,[1] and the current religions began to influence each other. The world was ready for syncretism. With Alexander it set in like a flood. He and his myrmidons, of course, brought the Greek gods with them, but they were quite ready to identify them with Babylonian or Syrian or Egyptian gods. The Seleucids of Antioch reckoned the reigns of their kings from the day when they severally bowed down before Bel in Babylon. In Egypt the assimilation of Greek with native cult became at last so close that the Ptolemies, like the the Pharaohs, could represent themselves as descendants of the old gods of the land. As for the Greeks and the Romans, it proved quite easy to identify Zeus and Jupiter, Aphrodite and Venus, Hermes and Mercury, and so on. The four last centuries of our epoch were centuries of syncretism on a gigantic scale. It was as general as the sea. Only the little rock of Judaism defied it.

What part did this strangely multitudinous and chameleon religion play in human life? There is no doubt that it was popular. There were temples everywhere and they were the usual centres of social life. In particular men spent their hours of leisure there. Here again there is more evidence for the Hellenistic than for the Persian period, and here too

[1] For instance, they made a great road from Susa to Sardis with a system of regular posts.

the climax was reached—if indeed the whole process did not lie—in the last four centuries. All the many social pursuits of the Hellenists were baptized into the name of gods. Gymnasia, amphitheatres, baths, even the haunts of public women, were more or less closely associated with temples. As usual, the people's pleasures betokened their social life. Their ways were as capricious, as heartless, as lascivious, as the ways of their gods. For serious men—and at length for others too—ethics fell apart from religion. Ultimately both in Athens and Rome poets lampooned the gods on the public stage. This is the second religious phenomenon of the time, and here again Israel was protestant; she believed that there was but one God, who ruled the world, and that He was righteous and demanded righteousness of men.

Amid this decay of popular religion men of devout mind sought sedulously for something better. They hoped that there was some cult somewhere that harboured truth. As so often, men found, or thought they found, what they sought. It was in the later part of this period that the esoteric cults spread that are to-day called 'mystery religions.' They present the third religious phenomenon of the period. As the term 'mystery' implies, many of them taught their adherents some secret that was the monopoly of devotees. The variety of the sources of these cults illustrates the desperate state of religion. The Orphic mysteries, for instance, grew from ancient Greek soil, the cult of Isis from Egyptian, of Attis from Phrygian, and of Mithras from Persian. This phenomenon needs no larger elucidation here, for it almost goes without saying that Judaism left it altogether alone. What others sought in these alien faiths, the Jew enjoyed in his own. A man does not go to look for what he has. On the contrary, the Jewish faith attracted some of the Gentile searchers. It is not probable that many submitted to circumcision, followed all the rules of Hebrew legalism and so became 'proselytes of righteousness,' but many began to haunt the synagogues and to enjoy their purer worship. These are 'the devout persons' of whom we read in the story of Paul.[1] The Jew seems to have looked at these 'inquirers,' as a modern missionary would call them, with mingled feelings. On the one hand, their coming to the synagogue was a compliment to his faith; on the other, there is something exasperating in people who patronize but do not conform.

The fourth religious phenomenon centres in the phrase *cujus regio, ejus religio*. It is, of course, a mistake to think that this idea first arose with the Protestant Reformation. The notion that a people, its ruler and its religion go inevitably together is of immemorial antiquity. When one race conquered another, this meant, at least sometimes, that the conquered race adopted the gods of its conquerors. When John Hyrcanus, for instance, conquered the Edomites (109 B.C.), he forced them to worship the God of the Jews. In not a few cases, the king was counted of the lineage of the national gods—himself a god, indeed. In our present period this was a particularly easy concept, for power obviously belonged not to the swarm of ancient deities, but to the ruler of the empire. So the Seleucid, the Ptolemaic and the Roman rulers all suffered or enjoyed apotheosis. The rule *cujus regio, ejus religio*, however, was not always enforced. Under Persia, as we have seen, there was

[1] e.g. Acts xiii, 50; xvii, 17.

no attempt to make the whole empire worship the gods of 'the Medes and Persians.' For the most part, again, the Ptolemies left the Jews to their own worship, though one Apocryphal book suggests an exception.[1] The Romans too, with their sagacity for government, were for long content to let the Jews worship as they liked. While they could not understand the fury that filled this little people when, for instance, Caligula wanted to set up his own statue in the Temple, so it was—and the Roman was willing to humour the fanatics. It was only when he found that his tolerance was all of no use that he pulled the Temple down and made Jerusalem a heathen city. Even then he let the synagogues of the Dispersion alone. The only determined attempt to extirpate the Jewish faith was made in the pre-Roman days of Antiochus Epiphanes (175-164 B.C.). This king, whose epithet perhaps means '(divine) manifestation,' did attempt to practice the creed *cujus regio, ejus religio* literally and completely. When he did so, the small Jewish people rose in mad revolt—and, wonder of wonders, as it seemed to them, 'turned back the battle at the gate.' But there was a battle all the time in a less dramatic form, for it was the general 'way of the world' to worship the gods of one's rulers. Why not, when it did not much matter what was worshipped anyway? Here again Israel was the one exception in its universe.

The marvel of the survival of Hebraism grows when we turn from the general world-situation to look more closely at the state of the Jews in particular. Of the situation in Palestine, whether political or religious, during the Persian period we know very

[1] 3 Maccabees.

little. On the political side we know that there was a fragment of the Hebrew race, clinging about its one city, Jerusalem, with one set of enemies, the Samaritans, on the north, and another, the Edomites, on the south.[1] This appears for the Edomite from several scattered references[2] and from the brief Prophecy of Obadiah, for the Samaritans from the records of Ezra-Nehemiah.[3] Twice only in the Persian period did Jewish hope flame up—once at the beginning of the period, when Zerubbabel and Jeshua arrived in Jerusalem, and again, about a hundred years later, when for once Judæa enjoyed the rule of a governor of her own race, Nehemiah—but each time the flame died down. For three quarters of the Persian period the Jews wrote no history. From their point of view there was none to write. Their God was alive, of course, but He seemed to be doing nothing much for them. They were only an insignificant bit of an alien empire—they, whose God was master of the universe!

With the coming of Alexander stagnation gave way to change, but for a century and a half the struggles over his empire brought no hope politically for the Jew. His country was now just a bone of contention between two Hellenistic states—and he was little asked what his own wishes were. Some have wondered that any Jew could ever write the Book of Ecclesiastes, with its refrain of 'Vanity of vanities! All is vanity'—

[1] Even before the Fall of Jerusalem in 586 B.C., the Edomites, under the pressure of the invading Nabatæans, had begun to leave their old haunts and spread into Judah.

[2] e.g. Lam. iv, 21f.; Ps. cxxxvii, 7; Mal. i, 4; Isa. lxiii, 1-6.

[3] *Before* the days of Nehemiah and Ezra, however, the Samaritans may have worshipped at Jerusalem and been reckoned part of the people of Jahveh. See p. 108.

but a historian may rather wonder that such books did not team. For from the point of view of an ethical monotheist, who took his creed practically, there was still no history to write. Then the victories of Judas Maccabæus and his brothers befell, and for a third time there was hope, and for a third time there is a piece of Hebrew history. Indeed, this time hope flamed higher, for it did look at last as if the one God were showing His power. History points out that the successes of the Maccabees were at least as much due to the growing weakness of the unwieldly Seleucid empire—fighting Parthia on the east and Rome on the west, and torn besides with internecine feuds—as to the dauntlessness of the Jewish heroes. But it did not seem so to Israel. God, affronted in His own Temple, was at last bestirring Himself. Straightway the slumbering nationalism of the Hebrews awoke, and for the greater part of a century Israel was politically free. But now her own rulers betrayed her. There is no sign of the rule of a righteous God in the story of the later Maccabees ! Yet still the faith held. Even when Jewish nationalism writhed to death in the grip of the Roman, the faith held. The closer one looks at the political fortunes of Israel in this period, the more one wonders at the survival of Hebraism.

This brings us to what is called the Problem Literature of Israel. It belongs almost exclusively to this period and the reason is easy to discern. So long as the Hebrew was a monolater, and so long as his god Jahveh showed himself able to further the interests of his own people, the question of the suffering of the righteous did not force itself practically upon the Hebrew. Had not Jahveh delivered him from

Egypt, led him into Canaan, established and maintained him there? And when any disaster befell Israel there would be an uneasy feeling that this was because it had displeased its god. The Prophets and the Dueteronomists clarified and enforced this feeling. They put all the woes of Israel down to Israel's sin, and declared unhesitatingly that if only Israel would turn to Jahveh, the one righteous God would send prosperity.[1] But now events gave them the lie. It was precisely the righteous in Israel that returned from Babylon—yet they did not prosper. Many of them presently fell into the conviction that it was useless to serve God—as the Book of Malachi shows. Even for the faithful the problem remained. Several attempts were made to answer it. Some, spite all evidence to the contrary, maintained the old doctrine—that suffering is always the consequence of sin. This is the finding especially of certain Psalms and of the Book of Proverbs.[2] It is possible to understand how it could be maintained if one puts oneself into a Hebrew village, especially during the Persian Peace. In such a village the frugal, industrious, moral family, loyal to Jahveh and to itself, would usually flourish, while the idle, spendthrift, dissolute family would tend to perish. But in the Hellenistic period the old doctrine was untrue even on this limited scale, as the Book of Ecclesiastes plainly says.[3] Palestine, like China to-day, was an almost continuous scene of confusion and war, and such days are evil indeed for peaceful and frugal peasants. They labour—and others enter into and

[1] See pp. 55f., 72ff.

[2] e.g. Psalms xxxvii, lxiv, and cxxv; Provs. iv, 10-19; xxiv, 1-22

[3] e.g. Eccles. ix, 2, 13-18.

destroy their labours! And, if any one looked at the world and not at a village, the old doctrine seemed altogether untrue. Israel might not be righteous before God, but it was much more nearly so than the Egyptian or the Syrian, and it was to these last that power and wealth fell. It was not wonderful that some gave the problem up in despair—as the writers of Job and Koheleth,[1] each in his own way. Yet, even when one reads the one really pessimistic book in the Old Testament, Ecclesiastes, one feels that this man spite all his bitterness, is no atheist. The writer of Job goes further. He makes an original contribution to the Hebrew doctrine of God. He discovered His inscrutability. The Prophets had said that they knew the truth about God. It was here that the strength of the 'prophetic consciousness' lay.[2] The writer of Job does not deny their knowledge, but he claims that it is incomplete. There are some things about God that no man can understand. This is the burden of the greatest chapters in the book.[3] Yet there is something more. Job's conclusions can be gathered into three simple statements: Sometimes the righteous do not flourish; here God's ways are inscrutable; none the less He is righteous. Christianity says all these things. There are two other items of thought on the problem in Job—one at the beginning and the other at the end. The scene in heaven dramatically poses a question that grew out of the Prophetic teaching that prosperity always follows goodness—Are men righteous just in order that they may be well off? Job vindicates righteousness against this suggestion of Satan. In

[1] The Hebrew name for Ecclesiastes.
[2] See pp. 93f. [3] Job xxxviii-xli.

modern phrase, for him righteousness is an end in itself. Yet the Jew cannot leave the subject there. For him God is not altogether righteous Himself if He leaves His servant scraping his sores on the dunghill. The 'happy ending' of the last chapter is an attempt to vindicate God. It amounts to this—Wait, and God will at last give prosperity to the loyal. The same answer appears in some Psalms.[1] In Apocalyptic the difficulty is faced in its acutest form—What if a righteous man *die* for righteousness' sake? The answer is—In the Resurrection God will vindicate him.[2]

There was yet another answer to the problem that Judaism strangely neglected. This is the doctrine of Vicarious or Altruistic Suffering, which, as we have seen,[3] had already appeared in the Exile. In this period there are one or two hints of the concept,[4] but on the whole it counted for little in Judaism. Christianity, on the other hand, from the first made it its own. It is not, of course, a complete theoretical solution of the problem of Undeserved Suffering, but it has proved sufficient in practice. Israel, on the contrary, has very rarely thought of herself as suffering for others, and suffering is not altruistic unless it is consciously and willingly so. None the less, though Israel missed so largely the deepest of answers to the problem, and though her own solutions were so inadequate, she won a great victory—her ethical monotheism, facing the unresolved problem, still did not falter.

It will have been noticed that it is impossible to

[1] e.g. Psalms xxxvii; xlii-xliv.
[2] This appears in Isa. xxvi, 19, and Dan. xii, 2, but bulks more largely in later Apocalyptic (cf. 2 Macc. vii, 9, &c.).
[3] pp. 76f. [4] e.g. 2 Macc., vii, 37.

describe the political threat to Judaism altogether apart from the social menance. Yet the latter needs examining separately, for here the Jew won, if possible, a yet more signal triumph. During the Persian period the chief danger came from the puzzling people who were later called 'Samaritans.' If they were descended from the mixed peoples whom Sargon had settled in the North,[1] they had once been polytheists, with Jahveh for one of their gods. Yet neither Nehemiah nor Ezra, with all their animus against the Samaritans, ever accuses them of polytheism, and there is some evidence that they had been used to worship at Jerusalem.[2] It is difficult, therefore, to say what the religious practises of the poverty stricken population of Palestine exactly was before the days of Nehemiah.[3] In any case the revival of the Jewish race did not spring from Palestine but from the eastern exiles. The great names are Nehemiah and Ezra, and these were immigrants.[4] In the lands of exile Israel, of course, could only survive by keeping to herself. Her policy could only be separatist. It was this policy that Nehemiah and Ezra pursued in Palestine.[5] Nehemiah would not allow the Samaritans to worship in Jerusalem,[6] and ultimately they built their own Temple on Mount Gerizim, as Josephus tells us. In their separatist policy Nehemiah and Ezra feared most of all the consequences of inter-

[1] 2 Kings xvii, 24ff. [2] Jer. xli, 5.

[3] The Elephantine papyri add to the puzzle.

[4] This is probably so for Zerubbabel, too, though some would deny that there was any return in the days of Cyrus and make Zerubbabel native to Palestine.

[5] It is likely that the materials of Ezra-Nehemiah have been wrongly arranged, and that Ezra is to be dated about 400 B.C., that is, after Nehemiah, not before him.

[6] Neh. ii, 20.

marriage and tried to forbid it.[1] The history of many peoples confirms their wisdom. If a child's mother were not a strict Jew, it was not likely that the child would be.

Whether Nehemiah initiated this policy of separatism or only reinforced and furthered it, it saved Hebraism. For there were only two ways in which Israel could survive—either it must attack and conquer the world in which it lived, or it must separate itself from it. As it was unequal to the first, only the second remained. The success of Nehemiah and Ezra appeared signally in the Hellenistic period. For throughout that period there was an insidious social menace, and in the middle of it a great ordeal. The word here is 'Hellenization.' From the political point of view the centuries from Alexander to Titus fall, as has been seen, into three parts—Hellenistic, Maccabæan and Roman—yet the one word 'Hellenistic' has been used for it, for the chief peril of Hebraism in these four centuries was social rather than political, and the word 'Hellenization' describes the social peril. It denotes the fact that beginning with the conquests of Alexander a Greek flood overwhelmed the world of the Bible. It did not belong, it is true, to the period when Greece was at its best, yet it was still Greek. The figure of a flood is used advisedly, for the same old soil remained beneath it, as ultimately appeared. But for Palestine and much else of the world the flood lasted for many centuries. The Greek tongue spread everywhere, Greek city-states dotted the world, Greek theatres delighted the populace, Greek literature engrossed scholarship, Greek statuary and Greek architecture were in universal vogue.

[1] Neh. xiii, 23ff.; Ezra ix and x.

The atmosphere of life turned Greek. It brought life, for one must do it justice—but it was Greek life. It also brought death. In Syria, where Palestine lay, every old institution died except one—the religion of the Jew. To return to the former figure, it, and it alone, breasted the Greek flood.

The struggle had three phases, at any rate in Palestine. The moot question in the first was 'How far can a Jew Hellenize and yet be faithful to Jahveh?' It is obvious that there would be very various answers to the question. The tendency to use Greek names soon spread and seems to have been general. Aramaic was now the language of Jewish daily life, but very many Jews learnt to speak Greek as well. Greek cities were founded, particularly in the region called in the end by a Greek name, Decapolis. In a number of the old Hebrew cities, Greek baths and Greek gymnasia were built. At last a High Priest erected a gymnasium in Jerusalem itself, and even sent gifts to the shrine of Hercules at Tyre. Against all this there was all the while impassioned protest. The so-called *Hasidim*[1] denounced every departure from old Hebrew custom and foretold that the Hellenization of social life would end in the Hellenization of religion. The second phase of the story ensued when Antiochus Epiphanes attempted this very thing. In the hour of final peril Israel rallied under the Maccabees and the issue was decided once for all. This does not mean that the peril was altogether past, but it does mean that the decisive battle of the campaign had been won. Herod the Great, for instance, might beautify the Temple with Greek colonnades—Herod Agrippa might even, in thoroughly Hellenistic fashion,

[1] i.e. 'the Pious.'

allow the citizens of Tyre to salute him as divine[1]—but the Jewish race, as a whole, had refused to be Hellenized.

A third phase ensued. At first sight its ruling question might seem to be the same as in the first phase, yet there was a real difference. The question was no longer 'Can a Jew who is of thoroughly Hellenist spirit remain loyal to Jahveh?' but 'How far can a man who is of a thoroughly Jewish spirit take over Greek ideas?' Here the chief impulse came from the great Jewish colony in Egypt. There, indeed, the last question had been the dominant one from the beginning of the Hellenistic period. As has been seen, the Ptolemies on the whole tolerated the Jew and even encouraged his religion. The leading illustration falls in the reign of Ptolemy Philadelphus (*ca.* 250 B.C.), for he patronized, or even suggested, the translation of the Law into Greek. The readiness of the Jews to undertake this seems to mean that in Egypt their common language was neither Hebrew nor Aramaic but Greek. As will appear below, at this time the Canon of Hebrew scripture gradually took final form. In Egypt a number of Greek books—some written in Greek, others Greek translations of Hebrew originals—were included in the Canon. These are genuinely Jewish in spirit, though some of them, notably the Book of Wisdom, betray the influence of Greek thought. At the very end of our period a great thinker, Philo, made a sustained philosophical effort to show that Hebraism was not only consistent with Greek philosophy but had from the first included its truths. To do this he had to allegorize wholesale, but this method

[1] Acts xii, 20ff.

was current in his days. It is not easy to say how far this attempt to incorporate Hellenism in Hebraism influenced Palestine, but it is certain that on the whole it was resisted. The Canon of Palestine rejected the Greek books. The Jew of Palestine rejected Philo and all his works. We don't know much about the Babylonian Jews at this time, but probably, as earlier in the days of Nehemiah and later in those of the Babylonian Talmud, they took the conservative side. It was the Christian Church that accepted the Greek Canon;[1] it was Christianity that sorted and assimilated the treasures of Greek philosophy. In the meanwhile separatism saved monotheism.

While the root reason for this achievement was the religious spirit of the Jew, its chief outward helps were two institutions. The first of these was the Temple. It has already been shown that the Deuteronomists set themselves to make this the one Hebrew shrine, and that a Prophet of the Exile, Ezekiel, looked to a restored Temple as the centre of a reformed Israel.[2] Here he differed from the Prophets that were before him, but what Prophets there were after him took his point of view. The burden of Haggai and Zechariah[3] is just the rebuilding of the Temple, and of Malachi the shame of the neglect of its worship. Behind the splendid oracle of the sixtieth chapter of 'Isaiah' there lies the notion that the Temple is to be the centre of the worship of the world. The returning exiles did not find it easy to rebuild the old shrine, but at length they did it. Nehemiah appears as the restorer of

[1] The additional books are gathered in the so-called Apocrypha of the English versions.

[2] pp. 86ff.

[3] i.e. of Zech. i-viii.

the city, but for him the city without the Temple would have been like a body without its head. During the centuries that followed the Temple was the centre of Hebrew unity. Before the Exile we have no detailed account of Hebrew ritual, but now it is exactly described.[1] The priestly caste took final form in three orders. The High Priest became the recognized head of world-wide Judaism.[2] We see him at his best in the famous description of Simon the High Priest in the Book of Sirach.[3] The sacrificial system reached its final elaboration, with a recurrent cycle of Festivals and one great annual Fast. To these the Jews poured on pilgrimage from all parts of the world. They came not only to worship but to give, and the wealth of the Temple was immense. Not a few of the Psalms are clearly songs of Temple worship,[4] and the writer of the Book of Daniel was no doubt describing the custom of many an exiled Jew when he pictures Daniel praying with his 'windows open toward Jerusalem.'[5] Many buildings have been beloved by many kinds of men, but probably none has been loved like the Temple. It was the symbol of a successful separatism.

At this time a new element became prominent in the Temple ritual. It is agreed that in Israel as

[1] Of course under the notion 'This is the way in which our fathers worshipped.' Consequently the ritual of the Priestly document in Exodus, Leviticus, and Numbers, is ascribed to Moses. And it is true that the ritual was no new thing, but the final stage of a very old, though continually changing and developing thing. Restoration, reformation, and development are not the same as invention.

[2] Though by no means always the worthy head—see I Maccabees, Josephus, and the Gospels.

[3] Ecclus. l.

[4] e.g. Psalms cxxii, cxxxii, cxxxiv, cxxxv, cxlvii, and cl.

[5] Dan. vi, 10.

elsewhere the original idea that underlay the offering of sacrifices was either gift or fellowship or both. In the references to ritual before the Exile there is little trace of a sense of sin. But the Prophets had done their work. It is true that at this time the Jews were probably the most moral people in the world. But if a moral man is also a religious man, and if he has learnt that God is righteous, he is deeply conscious of sin when he faces God. And the better he is, the more conscious he is of sinfulness. It is not likely that the writer of the Fifty-first Psalm was a bad man, as the world counts badness, but when he faced God he knew that he was evil through and through. God is 'of purer eyes than to behold evil.'[1] This Prophetic idea was now manifest in ritual. It included many sin offerings and guilt offerings.[2] More, there was the annual Day of Atonement. No one can enter sympathetically into its ritual[3] without feeling that Israel was now conscious of sin.[4] As always with a living religion, ritual responded to the things of the spirit and reflected them.

Yet the insufficiency of the sacrificial system has here its clearest instance. From the days of the great Prophets onwards its efficacy had been challenged, and the challenge is repeated in Psalms of this time.[5] Could it really be that the one God who ruled the universe found any pleasure in the blood of bulls and goats? It could not. The ritual is not to be justified on literal grounds but only on symbolic. Here it found partial justification. When a Jew brought an

[1] Hab. i, 13. [2] e.g. Lev. iv, 1-vi, 7.
[3] Lev. xvi.
[4] Some wish to make it refer only to sins of ignorance. I cannot agree with this. See *What is the Old Testament?* p. 216.
[5] e.g. Psalms xl and li.

ox or a lamb to sacrifice, he was denying himself one of his most valued possessions for the sake of Jahveh. A peasant had not many oxen or sheep. Further, the ritual of the Day of Atonement, in particular, did express vividly the awe-ful holiness of God—and therefore the terrible sinfulness of sin. Here we meet the numinous once more. But did the ritual adequately express the idea of forgiveness and reconciliation? Did it give any proper idea of the ground of forgiveness? Did the better kind of Israelite feel, as he saw the so-called scapegoat disappear into the wilderness, that he was now reconciled with God? It is here too—to widen the discussion for a moment—that the inherent weakness of Pharisaism lies. The Pharisees appear in the later part of the period, and seem to have been the lineal descendants of the *Hasidim* of its earlier generations. They kept all the many rules of the Jewish Law meticulously. They were not 'hypocrites' in the modern sense of the word. They did not, for instance, keep an honest front and steal in secret. They were 'superficialists.'[1] They did not know how to deal with evil motive—so they persuaded themselves that God would be content with outward act. Nicodemus, whether his story is historical or not, asked the right question; he did not say '*Need* these things be?' but '*How* can these things be?' The Pharisees have their names in every epoch and every race, and it is difficult to escape the subtle self-deceit that is their mark. They knew that every man has a sinful heart, but they did not see how this could be altered, so they concentrated on outward conformity to law.

[1] For this translation see Lukyn Williams, *Talmudic Judaism and Christianity*, pp. 67ff.

In the famous parable of Jesus, it is the Publican and not the Pharisee who tells the truth about sin.

To return to the Temple—it was only for the time being that it was the symbol of a successful separatism. It perished in A.D. 70, and Judaism has survived to this day. It has survived because all the while a better institution was growing. This was the Synagogue. It arose, not from any rule in any holy book or tradition, but from the mere needs of the situation. The Jew in the Dispersion could not worship regularly at the Temple; under the 'law of the single sanctuary' he could not offer frequent sacrifices at all; so he betook himself to the kind of worship that was possible. Perhaps the beginnings of the Synagogue run back to the groups that gathered in the Exile round such teachers as Ezekiel and Deutero-Isaiah, but the word is a Greek word and probably the institution was not full grown and regular till the Hellenistic period. The word practically means 'meeting-place,' and this tells what it was. The Jews of a given area met together in order that their common faith might survive. And, since they could not sacrifice, they did what they could—they read their sacred books, listened to their exposition, sang the Psalms of Jahveh and joined in His praises. They thought of all this as the 'second best'—yet here they were mistaken. To worship in these ways was better than to kill animals in sacrifice. It suited better the spiritual worship of the one true God. It did so not least because a Synagogue might be anywhere under heaven. Unawares the Jew had escaped from a localized religion. The Synagogue is a symbol of the kind of separatism that has saved Israel.

Two other things were inseparable from the Synagogue. One of these has already been named—the sacred books. It has been seen that the idea of a canon had ancient roots in Israel,[1] but in this period it grew into a great tree. In the Hebrew canon there are three parts—the Law, the Prophets and the Writings. Its arrangement differs from the Christian arrangement, which comes from Alexandria, and is of Greek-Jewish origin. The Jewish arrangement exhibits the growth of the Canon. Probably by about 400 B.C. the Law was authoritative,[2] by about 200 B.C. the Prophets, while the miscellaneous collection called 'Writings' did not attain its final form till the generation before Jesus.[3] Indeed in His time the place of one or two books in the Canon was still disputed.[4] The process of selection was gradual; for the most part the books seem in effect to have selected themselves. Probably the persecution of Antiochus helped, for he denounced death on any who retained their scriptures,[5] and a man does not die for a book unless he is very sure that it is holy. But probably the use of the Synagogue, and perhaps in some degree of the Temple, was the chief selective index. A book went into the Canon as it came to be read in worship, for it was only so read if it was recognized as the Word of God. And then a process began that went on for many centuries. It was necessary not only to read the book but to expound it. Many hearers, for one thing, were not too conversant

[1] pp. 31, 89. cf. Ex. xxxiv, 28; Josh. xxiv, 26.

[2] cf. Neh. viii. Some, however, think that this passage does not refer to the whole Pentateuch as we have it.

[3] cf. Prologue to Sirach and Luke xxiv, 44.

[4] For many further details see Ryle, *The Canon of the Old Testament*.

[5] 1 Macc. i, 56f.

with ancient Hebrew, and for them it needed to be turned into Aramaic. And for all it needed exposition. For the old law did not name every detail of current life, and men needed to know how it could be made to apply to current needs. Gradually two professional classes arose—the Scribes who made copies of the holy books, and the Rabbis who expounded them. No doubt these classes overlapped. Rabbis did not always agree with each other. For instance, just before Jesus' day two rival schools, of Hillel and Shammai, divided the allegiance of students. It was from this source that the 'tradition of the elders' arose. During our period it seems to have been unlawful to write this down, but later it took form in the gradually growing literature of the Talmud. Apart from exposition there was need for exhortation, and delight in it. So a kind of sermon arose in the Targums. For there have always been people who like sermons ! The Law could be a burden, but it was not always so. 'Oh how I love Thy law' is no solitary confession ; it is the glad cry of multitudes.

With the Synagogue and the Book there went the home, for a synagogue was, in the main, the meeting place of a local group of Jewish families. Here was another factor in separatism, and not the least important. In the Dispersion separatism was impossible unless it began with the home. Every faithful Jewish family insisted in being different from its neighbours. This was one great reason for the unpopularity of the Jew, for to be separate is to claim to be superior. And in fact the Jewish home was superior. It is not so much that at this time the Jew tended to monogamy. This is very likely though not easy to prove. It is rather that Judaism consistently protested against the adultery and prostitution that disgraced and degraded the Hellenistic world. So far as legal marriage went, the Greek and the Roman were monogamists—but they supplemented monogamy with almost unashamed vice. This does not mean that there were no chaste men and women in the world, but it does mean that their numbers were unusually low. Against the fearful laxity of its environment Judaism consistently protested.[1] And as usual, it had the women it deserved. The description of the perfect woman in the last chapter of Proverbs tells us what many Jewish women were. The most heroic story in the Books of the Maccabees is a story of a mother.[2] It is not accidental that more than one favourite book of the period centres in a woman.[3] The home was separatist and helped to save the race.

The Jewish account of the strange survival of Israel would have been quite simple—'The Lord takes care of His people.' But the Jew was a monotheist and he could not evade the question 'What is the relation of the one God to other nations?' His chief answer is in the Apocalyptic literature. To a modern reader this literature is unattractive and even repellent, at least at first sight, but this is rather because of its form than its teaching. It was popular among the Jews for five centuries—from Alexander to Bar-cochba. It was a monotheistic reaction to the seeming chaos of history, and it is not an accident that its vogue is practically coincident with the centuries of world-wide commotion that began with Alexander.

Perhaps the best example to begin with, if one wants

[1] cf. Mark vi, 17ff. [2] 2 Macc. vii.
[3] Esther, Judith, Susanna, and if it is of this date, Ruth.

to understand this literature, is the Eighth Chapter of Daniel, for there an Apocalyptist himself gives his own explanation of one of his own visions. First, the vision is ascribed to Daniel, a faithful Jewish leader of earlier centuries.[1] That is to say, the book is pseudepigraphic, for the real writer was almost certainly of the period of Antiochus Epiphanes, with whose persecution this particular vision ends.[2] Then the course of history is presented under a series of symbols—the Medo-Persian empire is a two-horned ram, Alexander is a he-goat, the Seleucid realm begins as 'a little horn' but it waxes 'exceeding great,' and so on. The exposition of the vision is given by 'a holy one'—that is, an angel—who tells Daniel what the distant and silent God is doing. Here are the marks of all the typical Apocalypses—they are pseudepigraphic, they are symbolic accounts of history, they claim to explain the strange ways of the one God with His universe. In many of them, however, there is another item. They not only portray the writer's past—they foretell the future. Here their characteristic account declares, still under symbols,[3] that the 'Day of Jahveh' is near, the Day in which He will give the victory to the righteous—that is, on the whole, to the Jew—vindicate His power, judge the nations, and set up an everlasting kingdom of righteousness that shall cover the earth. These ideas are found in every Apocalypse. Others occur in some Apocalypses but not in all. For instance, in the

[1] It is difficult to give his exact date, for the Book of Daniel makes him contemporaneous with Nebuchadnezzar and a king called 'Darius the Mede,' while Ezek. xiv, 14, 20, seems to treat him as of earlier date.

[2] See, for instance, Driver's commentary in the *Cambridge Bible* series.

[3] A fact that some expositors forget *at this point*.

first Christian century the idea that a 'Messiah' or Messianic king would rule the world in the name of Jahveh in the coming 'age,' was common and apparently popular. The New Testament gives us most evidence here.[1] The Old Testament, as earlier, has examples of the *idea*, though the *word* 'Messiah' itself does not occur of a *future* king in this period.[2] For this the New Testament finds parallels in such books as the Psalms of Solomon and the Similitudes of Enoch, but there is no uniform concept. For instance, sometimes the Messiah is human and sometimes super-human. The idea is by no means a necessary element in Apocalyptic.

It is at this late point that it is best to ask 'What did the Hebrews think about the state of the dead?' One answer, found in documents of all periods, is gathered under the term 'sleep.'[3] Along with this, though perhaps of different origin, there is the idea summed in the word 'Sheol,' sometimes translated 'the grave.'[4] This was the name of a great hollow or 'pit' below ground, where human life repeated itself in a vain, bloodless and shadowy way. Its inhabitants could be called 'shades.'[5] The concept is by no means peculiar to Israel,[6] but there are two fine descriptions of it in Hebrew literature. One[7] tells

[1] e.g. Mark viii, 29; xii, 35; xiv, 61; Matt. ii, 4. 'The Christ' is the Greek translation of the Hebrew phrase 'The Messiah' (Anointed). Both were *titles* among the Jews. It was among Christians that 'Christ' became a *proper* name, as in common use to-day.

[2] cf. pp. 74f. Zech. ix, 9ff., is the best post-Exilic example of the idea.

[3] e.g. Gen. xlvii, 30; 1 Kings i, 21; Deut. xxxi, 16; Dan. xii, 2.

[4] e.g. Gen. xxxvii, 35.

[5] e.g. Isa. xiv, 9.

[6] The Greek term 'Hades,' for instance, has broadly the same meaning.

[7] Isa. xiv, 9ff.

how even Sheol rouses from sleep to greet Babylon when its king and empire join the dead. The other[1] gives a kind of geography of the fallen nations that strew Sheol. In both oracles existence in Sheol is a vapid and dream-like recollection of life on earth. Yet its denizens are nations rather than individuals. This was natural so long as people 'thought in' nations and families rather than in individuals, and so far there is nothing distinctively Hebrew. But when Israel had reached the two concepts of ethical monotheism and of the value of the individual, the question was sometimes sure to arise 'Can the almighty and righteous God leave good men to the emptiness of Sheol?' The question was most urgent when His devotees were 'faithful unto death' in the persecution of Epiphanes, and it was then that the answer was most confidently given. Its most famous example is in the story of the Mother and her Seven Sons, told so poignantly in one of the latest books of the period.[2] It is probably to this story that the writer of the Epistle to the Hebrews refers when, after saying 'Women received their dead by a resurrection,'[3] he goes on 'and others were tortured, not accepting their deliverance, that they might obtain a better resurrection.'[4] How 'better'? Because they would not return to the earth as it is, but as it is to be after the Day of God. At this point the belief in resurrection becomes part of the doctrine of Apocalyptic.

Yet the belief in resurrection did not spring suddenly to birth in Maccabæan days. It is true that there are only two undoubted references to it in the Old

[1] Ezek. xxxii, 17ff. [2] 2 Macc. vii.
[3] i.e. in the stories of 1 Kings xvii and 2 Kings iv.
[4] Heb. xi, 35.

Testament,[1] but one of them is probably pre-Maccabæan. Again, the New Testament tells that there were some in Jesus' day who did not believe in a resurrection at all and who asked hard questions about it.[2] Again, the Apocalyptic books show that there was no agreement about details. Some held that all men would be raised for a General Judgement, the wicked returning to Sheol. Others held that only the righteous would be raised. In others there was a tendency to assert that all Jews would be raised to life and all Gentiles left in Sheol. Others, again, allowed that there were good Gentiles for whom there would be a resurrection. Then there was a movement of thought about Sheol itself. Some, at least, now thought that there were two parts in Sheol, one for the good, which was called 'Paradise,' and one for the bad, which was named 'Gehenna.' The second term was of Hebrew origin, but the first is Persian for a royal park or pleasance. This is probably very significant, for the Persian religion had a highly developed eschatology, which divided the good from the bad in the realm of the dead. It is very likely that in the development of the whole of Jewish Apocalyptic Persian influence was great, the Jew, as of old, borrowing what he could assimilate. On the other hand, it cannot be said that either for Apocalyptic as a whole, or for the Resurrection in particular, there was any one consistent and authoritative Jewish doctrine.

Apocalyptic is the heir of prophecy, and it is not remarkable that there are oracles that seem to fall

[1] Isa. xxvi, 19 (cf. xxv, 8); Dan. xii, 2. Such passages as Job xix, 25ff and Ps. xvi, 10f., may mean that the sick man expects to recover.

[2] Mark xii, 18ff.

halfway between the two,[1] yet with the likenesses there are differences. No typical Prophet could be pseudepigraphic. He did not ascribe his words to some ancient teacher, for he was sure that God had spoken to him direct. And the people believed this too. With John the Baptist and Jesus this phenomenon reappears. The people counted them prophets, for they believed that they had a word direct from God. Here the Apocalyptic teaching of Jesus differs from that of His contemporaries. The age thought that God had almost fallen silent.[2] It is not accidental that only a little of this literature was admitted into the Canon, or that what was admitted is so like prophecy. There is also a more subtle difference. The typical Prophet taught that God would vindicate wicked Israel if she *turned* to righteousness—the typical Apocalyptist that he would vindicate good Israel because she *was* righteous. It was the Baptist, not the Apocalyptist, who startled Israel with the old Prophetic cry 'Repent ye!' None the less the main ideas of Apocalyptic were true—Christianity too believes that God is in charge of history, that through all its vicissitudes He is working His righteous will, and that, spite all seeming setbacks and even failures, He will at last vindicate Himself in universal and righteous dominion. Apocalyptic made two chief mistakes—it expected the catastrophe and climax of 'the Day of the Lord' and the 'end of the age' in the immediate future, and it came too near identifying the righteous with the Jew. Early Christianity, using this literary form of the era of its birth, took over the first error but not the second. The Apocalyp-

[1] e.g. the Book of Joel and Isa. xxiv-xxvii.
[2] cf. 1 Macc. iv, 40; ix, 27; xi, 11.

tic vision of the Judgement in the Twenty-fifth Chapter of St. Matthew knows nothing of Jewish privilege.

The 'working creed' of Judaism at this time then fell into two statements—'God is caring for His own people, and He is going to judge the Gentiles.' In the Apocalyptic literature there are exceptions to both parts of this creed—occasionally, that is, it is admitted that very wicked Jews would be punished, or that very good Gentiles would escape God's wrath—but they are exceptions. Outside this literature the exceptions are more remarkable. In the Sixtieth Chapter of Isaiah, for instance, Jerusalem is to be the capital of the world, and all nations are to worship at it. It is true that the other nations are to come as the servants of triumphant Israel[1]—still they are to come. As seen above,[2] there are three great prophecies of Peace that some ascribe to this period; in these the nations are one with each other because they worship the one God. The allegory of the Book of Jonah is more remarkable still. Here Particularism is the servant of Universalism—Jonah, the typical Hebrew, is sent to preach to the Ninevites, the typical Gentiles. Yet this book itself shows how reluctant the Jew was to admit that the Lord might save the Gentiles rather than judge them. The Prophet is 'exceeding angry' because God spares Nineveh. There were protests, then, against the Particularism that goes so readily with Separatism, but they were unregarded protests. Very much in the Books of Psalms and Proverbs, again, or the story of Creation that opens our Bible, has no particular pertinence to the Jew rather than the Gentile, yet the typical Jew did not draw the universalist inference. It is the

[1] vv. 10-18. [2] p. 75.

teaching of Jesus, not of Hillel, that is universal; it was not Gamaliel but Paul who practised a Gentile mission. A Rabbinism that preached that every detail of the Hebrew law was of perpetual obligation, both on Jew and proselyte, could not save the world. Here Judaism made its 'great refusal.' In spite of the teaching of the Prophets, it made ritual sacrosanct as well as ethics. It would not be universal. None the less Israel survived and it survived by Rabbinism. There is a story that when the Romans were besieging the Temple, a great Rabbi, Johanan ben Zakkai, pretended to be dead and was carried into the Roman lines in a coffin for burial, and that he persuaded the Romans that true Judaism was not political, still less belligerent, but merely religious, and so the Romans allowed him to open a Rabbinic School at Jamnia. From Jamnia sprang the schools of Tiberias and Babylon, of Spain and Germany, and so on to this day. Whether the story is historical or not, it is symbolical. The Zealots who defended the Temple failed, the Temple disappeared, Apocalyptic dwindled away, and it became clear that the Jew had no political future. But Rabbinism survived, and saved Israel. This brings us to the final truth about Hebraism.

We have seen that in its earliest days Israel believed in a living god, and that the Prophets had taught that He is not only living but righteous. This faith has never failed. It has sometimes been said that in its final Biblical period Judaism was 'deistic.' If this means that it believed in a God who, having made the universe, lets it alone, it is untrue. Even the postulate of Apocalyptic—that God is all the time working His will among the nations—says so much. Yet it is true that the characteristic word for God at this period is 'holy,' and that this denotes His awe-ful separateness. There is probably no more numinous piece of ritual in the world than that of the Day of Atonement. And, while 'holy' was not just a synonym for 'righteous,' it did now include this concept. None the less there was the belief, not only that men longed for fellowship with God, but that God longed for fellowship with men. One of the signs of this is the growth of a series of concepts of intermediaries between God and man. One of these was the 'angel.' This was an old idea but now, probably under the influence of Persian thought, the idea developed. There were 'angels' for instance, whose names were known—Michael, Gabriel, Azrael and so on. In Hebraism their business was to bring news about God and His purposes to men. Yet now they were thought of as created beings, quite distinct from Jahveh himself.[1] Men yearned for a closer touch with God than this. So they spoke of 'spirit' and 'wisdom' and 'the glory,'[2] and 'word.'[3] With all of these it is impossible to say whether they are one with God or separate from Him. To use an old comparison, they are as much one with Him and as much separate as the sunshine is one with the sun and separate from it. They say at one and the same time that the one God is awe-fully separate from man and yet that He comes near to him. A Christian would say that they show the need for the Incarnation.[4]

[1] cf. p. 27. [2] In Rabbinic lore 'Shekinah.'
[3] In Greek '*Logos*.'
[4] For 'spirit' see, for instance, Isa. lxi, 1; Ps. li, 11; Joel ii, 28f.; for 'wisdom,' Provs. viii, 22-36, Wisdom i, 1-20; xxiv, 1-34; for 'glory,' Exod. xl, 34-38 (cf. p. 27); Zech. ii, 5; Isa. lx, 1; for 'word' and Logos, Ps. xxxiii, 6; Wisdom xviii, 15f., and Philo. 'The great Glory' is a name for God in the Book of Enoch. Other such terms for the manifestations of God are 'name' and 'face.'

Nor is this all. There were devout Jews who were aware that they had fellowship with God. Here the Book of Psalms is the great witness. Its hymns are of different dates and of different types, but it is impossible to read them and declare that those who wrote and used them were mere deists! The men who sang as they journeyed to the Temple from the ends of the earth did find God there; the people who sought the Synagogue to listen to the Law, did meet God as they listened to it; the men who taught the world to say 'The Lord is my shepherd' knew Him to be theirs. Hebraism has been saved by the Rabbi, and age by age the Rabbi, at his best, has led his people—through legalism, as he believes; in spite of it, as we think—into the very presence of God.

INDEX OF SCRIPTURE PASSAGES

Joel

Amos

Micah

Habakkuk

Zechariah

Malachi

The Wisdom of Solomon

Ecclesiasticus

1 Maccabees

2 Maccabees

Matthew

Mark

Luke

Acts

Hebrews

INDEX OF NAMES AND SUBJECTS

(*n* indicates a footnote)